ONE L

CALGARY PUBLIC LIBRARY

JLOO 9λ 9806

252. 03 R
Runcie, Robert A. K., 1921-
One light for one world

SOC. SCI.

Also from SPCK:
Windows onto God (1983)

Robert Runcie

ONE LIGHT FOR ONE WORLD

Compiled and arranged by
Margaret Pawley

First published in Great Britain 1988
SPCK
Holy Trinity Church
Marylebone Road
London NW1 4DU

Copyright © Robert Runcie 1988

All rights reserved. No part of this book may be reproduced or transmitted in any form or by any means, electronic or mechanical, including photocopying, recording, or by any information storage and retrieval system, without permission in writing from the publisher.

British Library Cataloguing in Publication Data

Runcie, Robert
 One light for one world.
 1. Church of England —— Sermons
 I. Title II. Pawley, Margaret
 252'.03   BX5133

ISBN 0-281-04334-5

Typeset, printed and bound in
Great Britain by
WBC Bristol

Contents

Archbishop's Foreword — vii
Acknowledgements — viii

LIGHT – FOR HUMANITY

T. S. Eliot — 3
St Hugh of Lincoln — 7
Biblical Study — 12
Christmas — 19
Blessing of the Oils — 26
Easter — 29
Ascension — 33
Encountering God: Why I Believe — 36
Encountering God: What I Believe — 44
Doctrine — 52
Religion and Humanity — 57
The Nature of Christian Belief — 63
Concern for the Spiritual — 69

LIGHT – FOR THE NATION

Zeebrugge Ferry Disaster — 77
Dresden — 81
End of the Second World War — 86
The Corrymeela Community — 89
The South Atlantic Campaign — 95
The Oxford Movement — 98
The Seventh Earl of Shaftesbury, 1801–85 — 103

The Ordination of Women	108
Morality in Education	115
Fighting Divorce with Faith	126
The Royal Wedding	129
Huguenot Heritage	131
Opening of Parliament	135
Church and State	139

LIGHT – FOR THE WORLD

One Light for One World	149
The Anglican Communion	152
Enthronement in Uganda	160
A New Presiding Bishop	165
Mission and Evangelism	170
ARCIC and Authority	175
Conception of the Blessed Virgin Mary	179
In South Africa	182
Meeting of Faiths	188
Thanksgiving in Shanghai	196

Archbishop's Foreword

'It doesn't do you justice', said a friend to one of my predecessors as they gazed at his recently painted portrait. 'It's not justice I need but mercy', was the reply. Part of me feels like that about this selection from the countless sermons and addresses which I have delivered over the past four years.

An archbishop cannot often enjoy the reassurance of a familiar congregation. Whenever he speaks he is in a different place, often with a strange audience, and faced always with daunting demands and expectations. Each time I prepare I seem to experience what T. S. Eliot calls 'the intolerable wrestle with words and meanings'. Yet I am grateful for the occasions and the people who drew me out on these themes. Their variety will surely prompt the reader to reflect what they might have said. I have often been reminded of the fictional character who says somewhere, 'I don't know what I think until I see what I say'.

Fortunately I have the support of an able, loyal and industrious staff. I am indebted too to many others who have been willing to advise me on what to say and how to say it. It is tempting for someone who has to preach often to make do with a handful of tried and tested pieces from the past. I am thankful to all whose imagination and thoughtfulness have stimulated me and kept me from taking the easy way.

The nervous chaplain who in my hearing once mixed up the grace before a banquet and prayed 'Lord, make us needful of the minds of others' said a good prayer for the all-purpose speaker. Prayer and preaching are inextricably linked: to preach without prayer is to utter words without wisdom. It is prayer which awakens hearts and minds to the love and truth of Christ. An archbishop relies a good deal on the intercessions of others. I am profoundly aware how much I owe to them.

Finally, Margaret Pawley has ordered my paragraphs and rescued my scribbles from obscurity. Without her patience and editorial skills this book would not have been written.

Robert Cantuar
September 1987

Acknowledgements

THANKS ARE DUE to the following for permission to reprint copyright material:

Darton, Longman and Todd, for the two sermons entitled 'Encountering God: Why I Believe' and 'Encountering God: What I Believe', reprinted from *Encounters: Exploring Christian Faith* (1986), edited by Michael Mayne.

Times Newspapers Ltd, for the article entitled 'Fighting Divorce with Faith', reprinted from *The Times*, 2 July 1984.

Faber and Faber, for extracts from *Four Quartets* and *Collected Poems 1909-1962* by T. S. Eliot, and for an extract from *Five Rivers* by Norman Nicholson.

Penguin Books Ltd, for extracts from *The Prayers and Meditations of Saint Anselm*, translated by Benedicta Ward. Copyright © Benedicta Ward 1973.

LIGHT – FOR HUMANITY

T. S. Eliot

IT IS TWENTY years since he died, and it is right that here at St Stephen's[1] we should remember and thank God for him. For thirty years this was Eliot's church; here he lived and worshipped and served. In this holy place his vision was kindled, his faith nourished, and his finest work inspired. You will have your own memories and impressions, and the reverence we all feel for Eliot and his achievement bring us together to celebrate a man who, in Edith Sitwell's stirring words, 'has talked with fiery angels, and with angels of a clear light and holy peace, and has "walked amongst the lowest of the dead"'. Words which remind us of the preacher's inadequacy today, for he must fall back on the words of a poet to do justice to the poet.

In the centuries since the Reformation the Church of England has been blessed with a number of outstanding men of letters. They are not men who always found faith easy, nor indeed always found life easy, but they are and have been men who have profoundly influenced the quality of their times. In the midst of sometimes unpromising ages they revealed the nearness of the Kingdom of Heaven. Last year we celebrated the bicentenary of the death of Samuel Johnson. In some ways it would be difficult to imagine two men more dissimilar than Eliot and Johnson, but at a deeper level there are things which bind these men together. Both had to fight their way through an experience of life, in many ways angular and difficult. Both knew the fear of madness, meaninglessness and death. Both lived their faith to the uttermost, and both bear witness to the grace and goodness of God.

Eliot was not only the outstanding poet and critic of his generation but a notable Christian spokesman. This was not accomplished without cost. At heart Eliot was always intensely private and reserved but he dedicated himself to public causes

---

[1] Sermon preached at the Requiem on 17 January 1985 at St Stephen's, Gloucester Road, to commemorate the 20th anniversary of the poet's death on 4 January 1965. The sermon was first printed in *Theology*, July 1985.

and spent himself in their pursuit. Eliot, the international American, who loved London, whose roots were in Europe, Dante's Europe, our Europe, believed with his friend George Bell[2] that the culture of Europe could not survive the disappearance of Christian faith and religious vigour. As prophet of a Christian Europe, Eliot travelled widely, lecturing and teaching, fostering a new spirit of confidence, cultural and religious.

More closely related to his central vocation as a writer, were Eliot's activities in support of the revival of religious drama. Encouraged again by Bell and Martin Browne[3] he wrote *Murder in the Cathedral*, first performed fifty years ago, so giving birth to a whole movement. In these and in many other ways Eliot involved himself deeply in the *public* life of Church and society, determined to make the contribution to the demands of his time which only a writer and intellectual of Eliot's calibre can make. In and through the commitments and activities there was always his prophetic sense of the futility and emptiness of a world which has forgotten the eternal presence of God. Remember the shock of the earliest poems:

> The winter evening settles down
> With smell of steaks in passageways...
>
> The morning comes to consciousness
> Of faint stale smells of beer...

and

> His soul stretched tight across the skies
> That fade behind a city block,
> Or trampled by insistent feet
> At four and five and six o'clock;

It is our world still.
But then come the visionary words:

> I am moved by fancies that are curled
> Around these images, and cling:
> The notion of some infinitely gentle
> Infinitely suffering thing.[4]

---

[2] Bishop of Chichester 1929-58.
[3] 1900-80; Director of the British Drama League, 1948-57.
[4] From 'Preludes', *Collected Poems 1909-1962*. (Faber and Faber 1963) pp. 21-3.

It is the work of the poet, the artist, the musician to recall us to a sense of that eternal unchanging reality glimpsed fitfully through moments of creative vision. This is the task, the search, the quest, to which Eliot was called and compelled. Striving, waiting, longing, yearning – this is the endless, *restless*, thread which runs through his life and work. The poet is a man caught between two worlds. Earthed himself in the impermanence and imperfection of time, it yet remains the task of the poet, and especially the poet who is also a man of faith, to catch those moments of vision, to show how another dimension of reality is opened to us without which the flux of time is barren and meaningless.

So 'This is the time of tension between dying and birth' and in Eliot we see gradually that it is in the birth and death of the Word made flesh, in God's coming to meet us in the here and now, that life's meaning and value are to be found. This is the moment of redemption; here is 'The point of intersection of the timeless With time.'[5] 'That moment of time gave the meaning,' and, says Eliot, 'our own sordid, dreary world [was] suddenly illuminated and transfigured'.

In his work there is no doubt this birth, this incarnation, is 'hard and bitter agony for us, like Death, our death'. At Christmas, says Thomas Becket, we 'both mourn and rejoice at once and for the same reason'. Moments of faith and vision, like moments of creation, come by the way that passes 'three trees on the low sky' – Eliot's own landscape, this. Here, at the cross, and 'in a lifetime's death in love, Ardour and selflessness and self-surrender' and in endless humility is 'the still point of the turning world'. This is the faith and the love and the hope which issue from despair:

> I said to my soul, be still, and let the dark come upon you
> Which shall be the darkness of God . . .
> So the darkness shall be the light, and the stillness the dancing.[6]

Out of the 'the meaningless practical shapes' of his own sometimes tragic and disoriented times, and with all the poet's agony and effort 'to express the inexpressible', Eliot has provided new generations with an enduring language in which to articulate

---

[5] From 'The Dry Salvages', *Four Quartets*. (Faber and Faber 1944) p. 32.
[6] 'East Coker' from *Four Quartets*, p. 19.

and enlarge our own fleeting experiences of faith and prayer. It is a prayer of longing; it must be also the prayer of waiting. There lies the serenity – that is Eliot's insight, too. Perhaps, above all, Eliot has taught us the value of silence and contemplation; not as a substitute for action, but as a precondition for constructive action. 'Teach us to care and not to care, teach us to sit still.' He has taught us that nothing of value can be done without sacrifice, without renunciation, without the long struggle of discipleship, without the prayer for God, the infinitely suffering God, to be God in his world. Only in such a way can we arrive at 'a condition of complete simplicity costing not less than everything'. I believe Eliot knew something of this too.

When Eliot quoted Mother Julian or *The Cloud of Unknowing* in the last of the *Four Quartets*, he was quoting writers who were then relatively unknown. It was Eliot who brought them into the mainstream of twentieth century literature. In a tribute to Evelyn Underhill, he spoke of her consciousness of 'the grievous need for the contemplative element in modern life'. It was a need of which Eliot himself was acutely aware, and his work has done much to make others aware of it; he has pointed the way towards redressing the balance between action and contemplation in our society. So, in this church where Eliot so often prayed, it is fitting that we should remember him as a man of prayer, a man who had a deep understanding of the need for the mind's anxious chatter to fall silent so the Word of God may be heard. By his own faithfulness in prayer Eliot helps us also to be faithful to that mysterious journey in which we are supported by angels and archangels, and all the company of heaven. For, as he reminds us, the work of prayer is always a mystery, linking living and dead, time past and time present, heaven and earth:

> You are here to kneel
> Where prayer has been valid. And prayer is more
> Than an order of words, the conscious occupation
> Of the praying mind, or the sound of the voice praying.
> And what the dead had no speech for, when living,
> They can tell you, being dead: the communication
> Of the dead is tongued with fire
> beyond the language of the living.[7]

May he rest in peace. Thanks be to God.

---

[7] From 'Little Gidding', *Four Quartets*, p. 36

St Hugh of Lincoln

IT IS NOT often that we celebrate[1] the eight hundredth anniversary of the enthronement of a diocesan bishop, and still less that such an occasion will draw together so large and diverse a body of people, representing different countries and different interests, as well as a variety of Church traditions. We give a special welcome today to the Bishop of Bruges and to a bishop and representatives of the diocese of Grenoble, the diocese from which St Hugh came, the diocese which saw the foundation of the Grand Chartreuse, the monastery to which he owed so much. This summer the present Bishop of Grenoble has given approval to a new and rapidly growing monastic family, the Sisters and Brothers of Bethlehem, who have drawn their inspiration from the rule of the first Carthusians of the eleventh and twelfth centuries. These women and men of our own day have found a source of new life and vision for an age which can seem far away from our own contemporary concerns.

In so many ways the world we live in is absurdly different from the world of St Hugh of Lincoln. The problems of the Third World, of space travel, of biotechnology – how unthinkable these things would have been in the England of King Richard and King John. But across the gulfs of time there is a quality which links us indissolubly with the past, and that is *holiness*, the theme of today's service. For there, in that elusive quality, so difficult to define but so immediately recognizable, we see something universally atttractive, something which breaks down barriers of time and space. In holy people we see a reflection of the light which shone in the face of Jesus Christ – the light of the knowledge of the glory of God. In that unquenchable light we see what human nature is called to be. After St Hugh's death in London he was brought back to Lincoln for burial, and it is said that throughout the journey the candles on his coffin were never extinguished.

---

[1] Sermon in Lincoln Cathedral on 29 September 1986, in celebration of the 800th anniversary of the enthronement of St Hugh.

It happens that in the providence of God, the diocese of Lincoln had another saint as bishop just seven centuries after St Hugh – Edward King. Men saw in him just that same graciousness and gentleness, that transparency of light. In the words of one who knew him:

> It was light that he carried with him – light that shone through him – light that flowed from him. The room was lit into which he entered. It was as if he had fallen under a streak of sunlight, which flickered and danced and laughed, and turned all to colour and gold.

The light which shines out in the faces of the saints is nothing less than the healing light of Christ. It creates in the saints a wonderful mixture of the qualities we sometimes think are opposed to one another: gentleness and firmness, humour and conviction, joy and capacity for sorrow. Sometimes, as in the case of St Hugh, it makes for a powerful combination of the inner life of prayer with the outward life of action.

This life is one which penetrates into the dark places of our world, and shines in situations where all seems lost. We see it today in a Mother Teresa of Calcutta or a Desmond Tutu of Cape Town: people saw it in St Hugh. He, too, had a special concern for the poor and forgotten members of society. He protected the rights of the Jewish community when they were particularly vulnerable. He took infinite trouble to give decent burial to the least outwardly important members of society. Kings were kept waiting at Rouen while he buried the poor, and the Archdeacon of Bedford had to cancel an important clergy lunch, since the Bishop was conducting the funeral of a brother of one of the cathedral masons.

Edward King was known throughout his life as one who could make immediate contact with the humblest member of his flock. I was once vicar of a country parish near Oxford where Edward King had been a curate. There was an old man there – universally loved and trusted; on his hundredth birthday he told me of his memories of Mr King, 'He got a job in Lincoln didn't he?' He would have liked that.

In one of the most notable incidents in Bishop King's life, he took over the role of prison chaplain here in Lincoln in order to prepare a young fisherman convicted of murder to receive the sacraments before his execution. He wrote later to a friend: 'He was most beautiful. His last (and first) communion on Sunday morning put me to shame. I felt quite unworthy of him. How little the world knows of the inner life.'

Yes, the inner life is a mystery largely hidden from the world. So it is in the life of the Carthusian communities which St Hugh shared in his native Burgundy and at Witham in Somerset. It is a life in which, in disciplined silence and solitude, in prayer and meditation, God can effect in men and women a transformation which can make them wonderfully free of human convention, wonderfully courageous in face of difficulty, wonderfully close to the whole of God's creation. We see St Hugh's independence of contemporary custom in the confidence of his relationships with women. He had none of that fear of the opposite sex which can sometimes mark the celibate. He invited women to his table, blessed them with affection and warmth, and would declare: 'God certainly deserves to be loved by women, for he did not refuse to be born of a woman, and thus conferred a special honour on all women. No man was allowed to be called the father of God, but a woman was granted the privilege of being God's mother.'

Some of the most extraordinary incidents in his life relate to his dealings with King Henry II and his contentious and treacherous sons. It was a household of violent and twisted passions which anyone might have been anxious about entering. Hugh had no fear of them. He won not only the respect but the friendship of the old King. Both Richard and John seemed to have felt a mixture of awe and affection for him. All his strength of character, as well as his sometimes caustic wit, are evident in his relations with these temperamental and tyrannical princes. If St Hugh had no fear of kings, it can hardly be supposed that he would have been afraid of archbishops. When my predecessor, Hubert Walter, came to visit him on his death bed, he suggested to the dying man that he might perhaps apologize for the many times he had crossed swords with the Primate of England. Hugh's reply was immediate, 'I do not consider that I should repent of angering you, but rather grieve that I did not do so more often'. There is no trace of weakness or compromise in the gentleness of the saint.

If saints are free and fearless, they often also enjoy endearing contact with creation. Not only St Francis had a special love for animals. Such stories abound in the history of Christian society – in sixth century Iona with St Columba, in nineteenth century Russia with St Seraphim of Sarov, in twelfth century England with St Hugh. These are not just quaint and picturesque anecdotes. They tell of love and reverence for the material world which has such urgent relevance to our problems today. One of Edward King's friends, seeing his love for the animal world, said of him: 'All nature was to him a burning bush aflame with God.' At the end of his life he preached a great sermon on the pleasures which God gives through the senses, 'the glory of thunder, the mystery of music, the singing of birds, the laughter of children ... O Lord how manifold are thy works, the world is full of thy riches'.

We often think of saints being revealed by drama and crisis, persecution, conversion of heathen nations, war and concentration camps; that was not the way for St Hugh or for Edward King who, in his Easter sermon in 1875 said this about saints: 'I want to see the English saints made in the old way – by suffering, diligence and labour in little things and in the exercise of unselfish, untiring love – quiet lives, lived away in holes and corners.' In the New Testament there is a special accent on patient enduring as part of sanctity. There is indeed a heroism about getting up every morning, scouring the pots and pans for the nth time, continuing with hope and courage the struggle against disorder and dirt; the patience which does the humdrum chores for love of the family; the patience which bears with sickness without spreading an atmosphere of gloom over the household. These common things deserve to be seen for what they are, an heroic way to holiness. One of the characteristic spiritual distempers of our time is impatience. People are not prepared to wait, not prepared to grow. They want satisfaction and results *now*. They seek short-cut solutions. Even sanctity has been sought through drugs which alter states of consciousness.

There is no substitute for patient endurance, and it is this unfashionable saint-building from which the Church must never be deflected. It is to be found in any parish, and one of the characteristics of the Church of England is that we have set great store by this simple, down-to-earth road to God. We stand in a tradition which sees the faithful performance of our daily Christian duty as more important than extraordinary insights or miraculous revelations.

We cannot claim to be alone or superior in believing in the virtues of the trivial round, the common task. The beauty of such holiness lies close to the heart of every Christian community. A great Russian archbishop in Paris between the wars declared that those walls which divide the Churches are never those which reach up to heaven. In holy people, like St Francis of Assisi or St Seraphim of Sarov, the unity of the Churches has already arrived. The same is true of St Hugh of Lincoln. In the planning and celebration of this anniversary year, men and women of very different Churches have played their part. Together as Christians we have acknowledged our common call to holiness. Together we recognize with thanksgiving the radiance of the saints and the splendour of the light which shines from their lives.

My final words for pilgrims – for a Church on the move – must be of holiness and hope. The saints we have thought about have reflected something of the glory of God in the face of Jesus Christ. But also they were people who built confidently for the tomorrow they knew they would never see: raising a cathedral, founding a religious community. Through a building like this they declare: 'Take courage for the future – God is real.' Could that be, deep down, why so many are coming to our cathedrals today however uncertain they may be? It should be so, and could be so in our parishes and communities. Holy people and holy places can speak to us in a language deeper than words for they do not need to pack their message into the capsules of ideas.

Take courage, God is real; we see his glory in the face of Jesus Christ and reflected in his saints. The call to holiness is a call to us all to share in this pilgrimage. Another holy person[2] speaks to us across the centuries: 'There is no stopping place in this life. No, nor was there ever one for any man no matter how far along the way he has gone. This then above all things: be ready for the gifts of God, and always for new ones.'

---

[2] Meister Eckhart (c.1260–1327).

Biblical Study

IT IS A great pleasure to be once again in this pulpit[1] at St Mary's and to be able to be with you at the start of another Vacation Term for Biblical Study. I have to confess that this is my first visit as President, but I am very conscious of your work and your distinguished history.

Miss Margaret Benson's initiative in beginning the Vacation Term in 1903 proved radical and far sighted. Women's higher education was still in its infancy – there were few opportunities available in *any* subject. And the days of residential summer schools and vacation conferences were yet to come. But Miss Benson saw what was needed if women teachers of Scripture were to be adequately nourished and encouraged, and her vision materialized in the first Vacation Term at Cambridge 82 years ago, with names like Headlam, Scott Holland, Moberly and Sanday on the Committee. The cost – £1.12/6 per week! From these beginnings you have developed and expanded. You have this year (as always) a demanding fortnight of courses and lectures to be given by scholars eminent in their fields of study. I only wish I could join you and sit at their feet myself.

Archbishops have all too little time for study and I am well aware that I am speaking today to people whose technical knowledge of the Bible and experience in communicating that knowledge are far greater than my own. Although I have been an Archbishop now for five years, I have obviously not become immune to flattery. That is why, when invited to give this Inaugural Address, I immediately accepted before wiser counsels could prevail! But I am also aware that the Vacation Term has never isolated rigorous scholarship and critical enquiry from loyalty to the truths and demands of the Christian faith. I take encouragement from that – though I am conscious that this proper and precious balance is again under threat.

---

[1] Inaugural address, Vacation Term for Biblical Study in the University Church of St Mary the Virgin, Oxford, 28 July 1985.

Today we live in insecure times. A growing fundamentalism is giving rise to one of the major obstacles to the effective communication of biblical knowledge: the belief that there can be only two possible attitudes to the Bible – to be 'for it' or to be 'against it': to make *everything* of it or to make *nothing* of it; to treat every sentence in it uncritically as inspired and saving truth, or to treat every statement in it as vacuous nonsense. That, of course, signals serious misunderstanding and distortion of the truth which I would like to examine. In doing so, let me explain in what sense and under what conditions I am *for* the Bible.

First, I am for the Bible when it is treated with reverent attention and understanding: when we recognize its right and power to address us and are open to receive whatever it may say. I am against the Bible when it is treated as a copious resource or store from which to draw sanction or even sanctification for any opinion we may hold or anything we may wish to say. When I use the word 'understanding' I have in mind the etymology of the word and the *posture* it suggests. To under-stand, to stand under (in German 'verstehen' – to stand in front of) suggests a posture of 'waiting upon', of being attentive, reverent, ready and eager to receive – to receive whatever may be told, disclosed or given. One might even call it an obedient posture – for the Latin root of the word 'obey' means 'to put oneself in a position to hear'. To understand does *not* suggest a posture of scrutinizing, analysing or weighing up, nor one of grasping, controlling or mastering.

When we speak of an understanding friend or of a patient partner we do not mean someone who can 'read us like a book', or analyse us or tell us what makes us tick. We mean someone who is attentive to receive, and even absorb, whatever it is that we may wish to tell or impart. I am for the Bible when our basic attitude to it is of this kind – when, to use an old and evocative phrase, we are prepared to 'stand under the Word', and discover for ourselves something of Coleridge's vivid experience of: 'God marching up and down the pages of the Bible, bringing it to life magisterially wherever he will.' An understanding friend does not remain wholly silent or passive as we tell what is on our mind. The friend will be listening with discrimination, seeking clarification at certain points, asking whether we mean this or that, and how one thing we say 'fits' with another. The posture of understanding involves the effort of discrimination. So it is also with the proper understanding of the Bible. There are questions to be asked, ambiguities to be sorted out, riddles and problems to be worked on and perhaps in the end resolved.

It is the special distinction of biblical scholarship in this University that its greatest practitioners have been motivated in their critical endeavours and achievements by a profound sense of being themselves addressed by the Bible, and by their need to discern more exactly the substance and meaning of what they were being told. 'The personal word', said Keble, 'is everywhere in the written word'; it is to this profound truth that their work bears witness. No one who has studied under R. H. Lightfoot or Austin Farrer, Christopher Evans, George Caird or Geoffrey Lampe, can be satisfied with the sharp distinction which is sometimes made between the devotional use of the Bible and its critical study. In the understanding of these men the two have been at one: discrimination and questioning have been the means to more exact and adequate receiving. And this indeed has been the spirit of the Vacation Term.

Such understanding of the Bible is worlds apart from using it as a quarry from which to select whatever stones may serve our own purposes or buttress our own position. In circles in which the Bible is well studied and well known, the use of individual texts in argument or exhortation can serve as a kind of shorthand – a *leitmotiv* to express a recurring and important biblical theme which at the moment is being overlooked. Speakers and hearers alike know that, taken by itself, the text is not decisive: they know also the broader context of theme and thought of which it is both a part and a reminder. The use of isolated texts as shibboleths to persuade or even manipulate the biblically ignorant, however, seems to me disingenuous in itself and a degradation of the Bible. And unfortunately, as biblical ignorance becomes widespread in our society, the opportunity for this kind of manipulation grows. In America some of the free-enterprise television evangelists are extracting millions of dollars from simple people by promises of instant cures and material benefits, and it is by this *selective* use of biblical texts that they identify themselves as Christians and invest their false promises with biblical authority.

We have not yet experienced this over here: but already, around and beyond the Christian fringe, there are an increasing number of small groups in which this kind of misuse of the Bible is reinforcing the power of a leader and the superstition of his followers. It is no exaggeration to say that in some of these groups the prestige and residual authority of the Bible is being put to demonic misuse. In some ways the misuse of the Bible is more dangerous to Christian faith than its disuse: it produces superstition in those who are persuaded by it and an aversion to the Bible in those who are exposed to it but not persuaded.

Secondly, I am for the Bible when it is allowed to speak to the imagination: I am against it when it is used simply as a container of doctrinal or moral truth. I am for it when it is seen as what Blake called the truth that is on the wing. Modern scholarship has been much concerned with the fact that a great deal of the Bible is *narrative* – the telling of stories of what happened, rather than the prescription of ethics or dogma. More than half of both Testaments consists of lengthy accounts of 'what happened', either in the ancient history of Israel or in the life of Jesus and the early Church. Why this is so, is clarified if we think about the function of narrative in ordinary life. We use narrative, we tell what happened, when general statements or descriptions fail to convey what we mean. Perhaps a retired colleague asks us about the new principal – 'What's he like?'. We search for words, 'He's rather timid – or perhaps cautious. He's very quiet in manner: but I wouldn't call him nervous or insecure . . .' And then we find ourselves saying, 'Let me tell you what he did when so-and-so caused a scene in the Common Room.' To convey what precisely the Principal is like we tell a story about what he did. The meaning of the story cannot be conveyed adequately in the general description of the man as 'cautious' or 'insecure'. That is why we find ourselves telling a story about him.

It should be axiomatic that the meaning of a story cannot be extracted from it and conveyed in a few adjectives, any more than the meaning of a poem can be extracted and paraphrased in a schoolboy's précis. To receive the meaning one must hear the story itself or actually read the poem. Much the same is true of the narrative element in the Bible, and especially of what is, for Christians, the central saving narrative of the birth, life, passion and resurrection of Jesus Christ.

That narrative must be allowed to speak for itself. We may offer hints or pointers to its meaning: but those hints or pointers cannot be substitutes for the narrative itself. We must not be so concerned in teaching or preaching to point to the ordered doctrinal or moral implications of the story that the story itself fades from view. That the story itself should be told and become known and remembered (at least in outline) seems to me the first priority of biblical teaching, whether in our schools or churches. It would be vain, pretentious and impoverishing to offer general statements of the meaning of Christianity as a substitute for attention to the biblical story of our salvation. Few people are led to belief in God or an understanding of his ways by reading books of theology, but many owe their faith to stories, not only the stories of the Bible, but the stories told by novelists and poets and friends.

Thirdly, I am for the Bible when it is presented and received as true: I am against it, or at best indifferent to it, when it is presented and received as improving fiction. Of course the Bible contains many different kinds of literary material expressing many different images, outlooks and interpretations. Some kinds of material, such as exhortation, cannot be either true or untrue and other kinds, such as myths or parables, actually present themselves as improving or illuminating fiction. Also there are factual statements which are clearly untrue, if only because they are contradicted by other statements in the Bible. But beyond all these qualifications there is a fundamental question of truth or improving fiction which cannot be avoided – and certainly not by the argument that fiction itself can be true: it can show what the world is like; it can be true to life.

We recognize fiction as true to life only because we already know what life is like: true-to-life fiction articulates what we already feel in our bones; it makes explicit what is already implicit in our consciousness. Now the essential narrative of the Bible as Christians understand it is *not* 'true-to-life' – it is anything but. It is paradoxical. It is contrary to anything that one might or could have expected. It is about an act of God so generous to mankind that if any man had expected it he would have been grossly deluded and unpardonably blind to his own alienation from God. If that act of which the Bible tells *happened*, then the Bible is essentially and savingly *true*; if it did not happen then the Bible is essentially *false* and not true in any important sense at all.

I recognize, of course, that the act of God of which the Bible tells, reaches us through the veil of flesh, the mists of history and the ambiguities of language. The historical event of which that act of God is the meaning, cannot be discerned with absolute certainty or detailed clarity. But it is idle to deny that the truth of the Christian Bible stands or falls by the occurrence or non-occurrence of certain things which, if they occurred, are decisive for man's destiny and salvation.

Truth compels us to recognize that we are faced in God and in the Bible with a reason, a logic, a reasonableness which is different from that which we instinctively employ. For God's thoughts are not our thoughts nor are our ways his ways. He does a work, a strange work, a strange act, and all that is promised for us in the cross and resurrection. That reality and that reason of God lie crosswise at the heart of his universe – and our use of Scripture at its best will help us to become familiar with that reason and that logic which are those of eternity.

It will be evident, I hope, that I am well aware both of the importance of good biblical teaching and of its difficulty. Without doubt, there are pitfalls for the student and the teacher on every side. But let me finish with one piece of encouragement from my own experience as a preacher. No sermon proves more effective than one over which one has wrestled and struggled: no exhortations prove more powerful than those which have been wrung out of the preacher. In biblical teaching the struggle which is involved for the teacher may well suggest more powerfully than words the importance of the subject, and the uncertainty of the teacher at various points may well encourage those who learn from them to apply their own minds. Those who struggle with difficulties have an authority and appeal which is lacking in the self-assured and smoothly confident. Certainly it would not be surprising if the most effective biblical teaching and scholarship came from those who are most aware of the difficulty of the subject, and of their own limitations and need for guidance.

There is also much spiritual benefit to be had from the scholarly discipline of handling words and language with precision and sobriety. Care in our use of words and with the accuracy of our expression is a preparation for the attentiveness which is at the heart of contemplative prayer. It also fortifies us in our resistance to the wild and extravagant talk which is beoming more prevalent in our western societies. The telegraphic speeds with which our public communications systems work do not encourage subtlety or balance or time to do justice to the complexity of problems. They do encourage slogans and simplistic explanations, which can contribute to a climate of thought in society which is dangerously glib. As Dag Hammarskjold said: 'Respect for the Word is the first commandment in the discipline by which a man can be educated to maturity, intellectual, moral and spiritual.'

It is, of course, for these very reasons that you are here in Oxford today. I pray that in the fortnight ahead you will discover new difficulties to wrestle with and fresh ideas to absorb – but also renewed faith in the Bible's abiding truth and living power. So, may you 'continue in what you have learned and have firmly believed, knowing from whom you learned it and how you have been acquainted with the sacred writings which are able to instruct you for salvation through faith in Christ Jesus'[2]. Amen.

---

[2] 2 Timothy 3.14f.

Christmas

THE LIGHT SHINES on in the darkness and the darkness has never overcome it.[1]

Tonight[2], rather than perplex you with philosophical conundrums, or strain after politics or social relevance, I want to ponder the good news of the birth of Jesus Christ given to us in just one of the Gospels, that written by St Matthew. I intend to cut through the ecclesiastical tinsel, however beautiful, however edifying, like the animals who were placed about the crib by St Francis, and the legends of the three kings. I want to take you back to St Matthew's own account of the birth of our Lord, in the conviction that just as it has sustained hope through many centuries of darkness, so now it brings us encouragement of the Light which shines on in the darkness and is never overcome by it. This is the basis for the celebration of Christmas, not only as a climax today to the season of expectancy and preparation, but also as a new beginning with the freshness and power to dispel depression even in the dark days to come, through which all have, sometime, to travel.

If we go to the pages of St Matthew with the wrong expectations, we can be disappointed and confused. If you were to hear the verse 'Humpty Dumpty sat on a wall, Humpty Dumpty had a great fall', you would immediately recognize it as a nursery rhyme. You would not ask historical questions about it although this rhyme is probably, in fact, connected with some incident in English history (precisely which incident is disputed). We know that we should enjoy the song without expecting it to yield very much sober or precise historical data. St Matthew's story of the birth of Jesus is certainly not in the category of nursery tale, but neither can it be understood as simple biography. It is a meditation on the person and significance of our

---

[1] John 1.5.
[2] Sermon on Radio 3, Christmas night, 1983.

Lord Jesus Christ. The more closely you study his text, the more you appreciate with what superb artistry and colour St Matthew introduces us to Jesus, who is presented as the one who is the climax and the goal towards whom history has been pointing and moving. But he is not only a climax; he is also a new beginning.

St Matthew follows St Mark in many places, but like Luke, he finds that he can share many of his deepest convictions about Jesus by telling the story of his birth (which Mark does not). He is writing from the heart of a Christian community alive with the experience of the resurrection. It is in the light of that event that St Matthew meditates on the person of Christ and his birth. That is not to say that he did not weave authentic historical elements into his narrative. We need not doubt that Jesus Christ was born in Bethlehem in the days of Herod the King, but if we are looking just for biographical information, we have missed the truth St Matthew means to convey to us, and we have missed the riches of his gospel.

In identifying St Matthew's message, we are fortunate in having vital clues to his meaning in the Old Testament. Our gospel writer, like other Jewish Christians in the earliest days of the Church, was steeped in the imagery of the Old Testament. As St Matthew meditates on the person of Jesus Christ, ponders the significance of his death and resurrection and seeks to convey the Christian experience of the living Lord, he naturally draws on the treasury of images provided by the Old Testament. Doubtless he understood many passages of the Law and the Prophets in a way not foreseen or intended by their authors, but if we want to understand what St Matthew is trying to tell us, we have to be alert to the connections he establishes between his narrative and the Jewish Scriptures.

The gospel begins with its title in verse 1: 'The Book of the Generation of Jesus Christ, the Son of David, the Son of Abraham.' Just in that small verse, Matthew tells us a great deal about his purpose and theme. The word 'generation', in Greek 'geneseos', reminds us of the very beginning of the Scriptures, the first book of which is, of course, Genesis. Jesus Christ sums up the past. The past has been moving towards him, has been pointing to him, though this can only be seen with eyes enlightened by the resurrection faith. Jesus is the Son of Abraham, to whom God made the promise: 'In thy seed shall all

Christmas

the nations of the earth be blessed.'[3] He is also the Son of David, to whom another promise was made: 'Thy throne shall be established forever . . . I will set up thy seed after thee . . . I will be his father and he shall be my son.[4]

St Matthew immediately relates Jesus Christ to the drama of history. Our Lord teaches truth which is good for all time, but he is also in himself a great historical event. This sense of the profound significance of the historical drama which is played out in time is characteristic of Christianity. An illustration of this is very fresh in my mind, since I have just returned from a visit to the Christian Church in China. The very first Jesuit missionary to penetrate Peking brought with him, as a gift that fascinated and intrigued the Emperor, a mechanical clock which struck the hours. Chinese culture put the accent on achieving a steady state of harmony and balance. Time seems almost an illusion. With the arrival of the missionaries and the first chiming mechanical clock, you have the arrival of a different sense of history – history as a drama moving to the climax of the coming of Jesus Christ.

The theme of Jesus Christ, climax and genesis, is developed in St Matthews's genealogy which runs from verse 2 to verse 17. There are differences between the line of descent sketched for us by St Matthew and that given to us by St Luke. This is one of the many details which should alert us to the symbolic character of the genealogy, which is certainly very far from being marked by a merely antiquarian interest in family trees. St Matthew makes many oblique but telling statements in this passage about the significance of our Lord for the whole past history of the Jewish people and beyond. The important turning points in the history of the people of Israel are presented as the journey of Abraham, the reign of King David, and the Exile. The genealogy suggests that all these movements culminated in the life, death and resurrection of Jesus Christ. But he is not the descendant merely of the chosen race and the inheritor of the promises given to Abraham and David. Great significance is attached to some rather surprising characters in this list, notably Rahab the harlot of Jericho and Ruth the foreigner. Jesus Christ is the descendant of aliens and sinners, and rose and lives for them also.

Matthew explicitly states that each of the three periods into

---

[3] Genesis 22.18.
[4] 2 Samuel 7.12f.

which he divides the history of Israel comprises fourteen generations; a clue to the symbolic character of his interest in this number probably lies in the lunar calendar. Just as there are fourteen days from the new moon to the full moon, and another fourteen from the full moon to the end of the month, so one can see Abraham as a beginning, David as a climax, and the Exile marking the close of the cycle. Christ, therefore, appears as a fresh climax. There are other ways of penetrating to the significance of the genealogy. The conclusion of these subtle and finely textured pieces of work however is always the same: Jesus Christ is both the climax and a new beginning.

The next section begins at verse 18 and continues to the end of the chapter. Mary is found with child of the Holy Ghost and an angel of the Lord appears to Joseph in a dream saying: 'Joseph, thou son of David, fear not to take unto thee Mary thy wife, for that which is conceived in her is of the Holy Ghost.'

One of the great religious controversies of the past 100 years and more has centred upon the virgin birth. It is easy to ask the wrong questions. People of our own day often ask for scientific evidence for or against the virgin birth as a biological marvel. Such evidence obviously does not exist, and Matthew is not interested in the question. He is meditating on the significance of Jesus Christ and we can come closer to his meaning once again if we look at some of the parallel stories in the Old Testament, with which Matthew's own mind was stored. The story of the birth of Samson in the thirteenth chapter of the Book of Judges is one such. His mother was 'barren and bear not. And the Angel of the Lord appeared unto the woman and said unto her – Behold now thou art barren and bearest not, but thou shalt conceive and bear a son . . . and he shall begin to save Israel out of the hand of the Philistines.' At the very simplest level Christ, like Samson, is God-sent. If we are guided further by the Old Testament in our meditation on the story of the virgin birth, however, we shall be led to raise questions about the long tradition which we have inherited which sees virginity as something desirable, since it preserves a person from the defilement of sexual relations. St Augustine said: 'All flesh which is born of sexual union is sinful flesh.' Against the background of the Old Testament, however, the meaning of the virgin birth appears to be rather different. Not to have children was a very great affliction, and there are many stories, like that of Samson which we have just mentioned;

the one about Abraham's wife Sarah, shows this very clearly. The heart of the story about the virgin birth is both assertion that Jesus Christ is uniquely related to God himself, and that God is able to bring life out of emptiness. The early Christian community knew from its own experience that life had come from the empty tomb. One of the ways in which this experience was expressed is in Jesus's birth from the empty womb.

It is missing the point altogether to speculate whether the word 'Virgin' in Greek or Hebrew can be rendered simply as young woman. This has been a way in which some commentators have attempted to remove the suggestion of abnormality from the story of the birth of Jesus Christ. The truth of the story needs a Virgin Birth. I am sympathetic to those Christians who are embarrassed by the suggestion that Jesus was born in what they see as an abnormal way. It is foolish to erect unnecessary stumbling blocks to faith, but the heart of our faith is that God acts in history and that he brings new life out of barrenness. We do not believe that God has simply wound up the world and set it ticking by itself. We do believe that in Jesus Christ God has come into the world in a quite unique way. The virgin birth is of very great significance as an expression of fundamental Christian beliefs about God and the person of Jesus Christ. Let no one be mistaken: this *does* challenge what most of our contemporaries believe to be the case about the world and its history. Our Christian conviction that God does act even in death and emptiness to generate new life is one of the reasons why Christians have a hope which has never been quenched in the 2,000 year history of the Church; a hope in a light shining in the darkness, which stands in contrast to the depression and fear of those who are oppressed by a world whose cruelty and injustice simply has to be borne as part of the inevitable nature and order of things. Jesus Christ does not just stand for certain moral values and truths about human living. His coming was an historical event in which all human history finds its centre.

Thus far St Matthew concentrates on Christ as the climax of the past. With the visit of the Wise Men from the East, we have more of the sense of Christ as a new genesis. God's promises were first made to Abraham, to David and to the Jewish nation. This is the kernel of the story, and once again, it may be interesting but it can also miss the real point to speculate on times and seasons. King Herod actually died in 4 BC, so tying the visit of the Wise Men to his reign suggests that our Lord was actually born before the start of what we have designated the Christian Era. Much also has been made of the star; and there are various theories identifying it with Halley's Comet, which is believed to have appeared in 12 BC, or with some meteor. There may also be some parallel with Rabbinic writings or the Book of Kings which described the visit of the Queen of Sheba, who was guided to King Solomon by a star. Here again, I believe we are given a picture by St Matthew, drawn from the Old Testament, which reveals to us not only the global significance of Jesus Christ for all nations, but also his cosmic stature. Here also there are references to the death and resurrection of our Lord in the light of which Matthew ponders on his beginnings. The Wise Men bring gold, frankincense and myrrh. Matthew is constantly drawing parallels between our Lord's birth and death and resurrection. This was superbly captured by T. S. Eliot in his poem 'The Journey of the Magi'.[5] The Magi wonder

> were we led all that way for
> Birth or Death? There was a Birth certainly,
> We had evidence and no doubt. I had seen birth and death,
> But had thought they were different; this Birth was
> Hard and bitter agony for us, like Death, our death.
> We returned to our places, these Kingdoms,
> But no longer at ease there, in the old dispensation,
> With an alien people clutching their gods.
> I should be glad of another death.

This intimacy between birth and death in St Matthew's account quickly receives the most brutal illustration. Herod seeks the young child to destroy him; the King slew all the male children in Bethlehem under two years old. There was weeping and great mourning. The Christian faith is impregnated with hope, but it is not a religion of sunny optimism. There is much darkness in the world that wars against the light. There is in every century a conflict between those who wish to dominate and force, and those who see the only perfect and enduring peace in acknowledging God as the giver of life and seeking to overflow with God's own generosity and love as we see them in the face of Jesus Christ, God's son. We celebrate the birth of the child at

---

[5] *Collected Poems 1909-1935*, p. 108.

Bethlehem in a world still apparently dominated by the mailed fist. The contest always seems so unequal – the child on the one hand; the mailed fist on the other. But we are convinced that the light shines on in the darkness and that the darkness can never overcome it. The kingdoms of the world built on violence and injustice do not endure. Herod dies and the child comes, like the Israelites in the story of the Exodus, out of Egypt, back into the land of Israel.

It has been possible to share only little of the almost inexhaustible significance of the two chapters in which St Matthew presents, in a lively and vivid manner, the faith by which Christians have lived and died, the faith of the risen Lord. These twelve days of Christmas are a period in the year when we are invited to mull over these pictures and meditations. We are to enter into them profoundly, so that after the most careful and reverent study, thought and prayer, we may open doors in the words and pictures Matthew has given us – doors through which the risen Christ himself can come. We do not read these stories out of idle curiosity in quest of mere information about the biography of some celebrated historical character. We read to the end that Christ himself can enter into us, be born and grow inside us, tranforming us into lights in the darkness. We pray that under the inspiration of the child of Bethlehem, we may shine in a way which will lead others to the true source of peace and joy. May God bless you this Christmas time – you and all those whom you love.

Blessing of the Oils

THIS MAUNDY THURSDAY Eucharist[1] has many themes for our thoughts. I would like to speak of the healing ministry of the Church, and to begin with a personal experience of my recent visit to India.

Some of you may know the famous Mission Hospital at Vellore. Its origin lies in the work of Dr Ida Scudder and her vision of the unity between the healing and the teaching of the gospel. Nowadays this hospital is a great compound with marvellous achievements in hi-tech medicine that could rival the facilities of a London hospital. In recent years they have felt the need to recover something of the original vision of their founder so a whole section of the hospital now provides a place where a sick person can come and be ministered to by their own family, by friends, by a local pastor. It is called community medicine. In fact it is an expression of the unity we find in the New Testament between healing and salvation: 'The Spirit of the Lord is upon me because he has anointed me to preach good news to the poor . . . and recovering of sight to the blind.' In our intercession at the Eucharist we pray: 'Comfort and heal all those who suffer in body, mind or spirit . . . and bring them the joy of your salvation.'

In the modern world the art of healing, the art of the doctor and the nurse, is often seen as a purely technical process. Salvation, on the other hand, is seen as something which concerns not the body but the soul – a matter for clergy or counsellors. But in the New Testament the same Greek word is used for healing and salvation: here, body and soul are as one. Someone once said to me: 'You should remember that the Christian congregation should be a primary unit for healing in society.' Do we think much in that way? If you look at the New Testament it certainly seems what was intended. Otherwise how can the Church be called the body of Christ? St Paul clearly sees

---

[1] Sermon at the Liturgy of the Blessing of the Oils in Canterbury Cathedral on Maundy Thursday 27 March 1986.

the converse of this when he tells the Corinthians that many of them are sick and some have died because they have turned the Lord's supper into a centre of division instead of unity in one body. In ancient times the Sacrament was sometimes called 'the medicine of immortality'.

Behind that phrase lies the picture of the Church, with its life centred in this sacrament of the Lord's supper, as a healed and healing community in which the healing love of Christ flows out to heal the sicknesses of men and women. That picture is beautifully expressed in our epistle today: 'Is one of you ill? He should send for the elders of the congregation to pray over him and anoint him with oil in the name of the Lord. The prayers offered in faith will save the sick man, the Lord will raise him from his bed, and any sins he may have committed will be forgiven.' Here healing, forgiveness and salvation are all together as part of the normal life of a Christian congregation. This is what a Christian congregation is meant to be. Remember our Lord's words to the paralytic: 'Your sins are forgiven.'

Healing is part of our ministry as much as preaching and teaching are, for healing is an authentic sign of the presence of the Kingdom of God. We have a right to pray for it and to expect it, and those of us who are ordained should regard it as an essential and integral part of our ministry. But all ministry, says St Paul, is to equip God's people for work in his service. A whole congregation is called to be a healed and healing fellowship in which the healing love of God is ever at work to bind up the wounds of its members. And beyond this the healing work is spread out into the community around.

It is always an encouragement when you find in any parish the existence of a regular prayer group which has a special responsibility, either in church or in the homes of people, to bring them the Church's ministry of healing. But I am thinking of more than this. Doctors and health authorities lay increasing stress upon community medicine rather than upon the treatment of the individual sick. The purpose of medicine – it is often said – should not be just to cure the sick who come to hospital, but to do everything to create a healthy community. This kind of thinking should be both an encouragement to those who profess the Christian gospel and also a challenge to our so often feeble and faltering witness to it. When our Lord was in the midst of a crowded street, pressed in on every side by the jostling multitudes, a woman who was too timid to address him openly, touched the hem of his cloak, believing that she would be healed. Instantly the healing love of Christ was given to her and she was made well. If the Church is truly the body of Christ, then surely that kind of thing should be happening all the time. Whoever touches the Church – even in the most tenuous fashion, even in the midst of all the bustle and press of our business – should find that they have touched the source of healing.

The healing that we receive here as we meet in the Holy Communion is given to us for the sake of all our neighbours. That is why on Maundy Thursday I always think not only of the unity between healing and salvation, but also the unity of our fellowship round the altar and our service to the world. We are not meant, it seems to me, to put a fence around fonts and altars with passport and tariff restrictions. Christians, and particularly those who make the Church visible and available through the ordained ministry, are called to a difficult but wonderful task. We are called to combine dedication to our Lord, and the suffering and pain involved in treading with him the way of the cross – we are to combine this not with judging but serving the world, and enabling all those in the confusions and sicknesses of our time who reach out to touch the Church to find healing and hope.

We thank God at this Eucharist for the healing and salvation which flow from Christ. We pray for the renewal of that vision in our lives and in all the varieties of ministry which are undertaken in his name.

Easter

> Then were the disciples glad when they saw the Lord.[1]

THAT IS A very quiet Easter statement: they were glad to see him. The words do not suggest excitement or jubilation – still less a thrilling awareness of victory snatched from the jaws of defeat, or of tragedy turned into triumph. I dare say the disciples were also glad to see Jesus on that day in the past when they went to buy food in Samaria, and came back to find him still at the well were they had left him. It is the quiet gladness of reunion with a friend.[2]

All the Gospel stories of the first Easter end on this note of quiet gladness. Some also include the quiet, almost homely, note of a meal shared with Jesus – at Emmaus, in the upper room, on the lake shore. Of course, there are other notes too – of doubt or uncertainty, and of a continuing wonder that, after all that happened on Good Friday, they can be once more in his company. But even the doubt does not amount to aggressive scepticism, and even the wonder is restrained. Throughout the stories there is a notable quietness both in what happens, and in the way the disciples respond. The stories of the first Easter are surprising – they are not what we might have expected. It was not until thirty years or more after that first Easter that these stories were written in their present form. In the intervening years the Church had 'gone public' on the enormous significance of Jesus' resurrection. So any Christian who simply imagined, thirty years later, what the first Easter must have been like was bound to imagine events far more dramatic, far more stirring and exciting than those quiet happenings the gospels report. So I take it as fact that the first experiences of meeting the risen Christ were suffused with a personal and even private gladness. The risen Christ was first experienced, not in wind or fire or earthquake,

---

[1] John 20.20.
[2] Sermon in Canterbury Cathedral at the Sung Eucharist on Easter Day, 30 March 1986.

but in a still, small voice of calm. He came not as the lightning flash, but as the quiet dawning of a new day. And his words to his friends were quiet words of peace.

In our celebrating of Easter in the world today it is not easy to recover the quietness of the first Easter. We are confronted, at home and abroad, by the dark, demonic dimensions of human nature which can cause the most resilient spirit to quake and quiver. We must, as Christians, be the sworn foes of vicious assault and callous cruelty; of persecution, poverty and powerlessness. We must be restless and unhappy when the freedom of millions is thwarted by hunger or discrimination. Our Christian confidence will be tested again and again by the will of our practical action in these heart-breaking tragedies. But we should also be aware that our witness to the Christian faith is not exhausted in achieving social order or equality or material betterment. Communities can be well fed and prosperous, highly cultured, and liberal and democratic in their institutions – and still be full of self-indulgence, indecent luxury and domestic tragedy.

We who are Christians have the difficult task of caring for all these aspects of freedom and justice, and joining with others, Christian and non-Christian, people of any or no religion, in contending against those evils which scare and scar the human scene. And yet we must keep before ourselves, and others, the truth that our security and strength lie with God – a security given by Christ, a quiet strength which comes from outside ourselves, and is unaccountable by the world's circumstances and understanding. This is the real source of our joy, hope and peace: it is the mark of Easter faith. 'If then you have been raised with Christ,' says St Paul, 'seek the things that are above, where Christ is seated at the right hand of God.'

In a world where even trivial events generate many words and much noise, and where no truth can be firmly believed and safe among our treasures unless it is asserted stridently, aggressively, controversially – in such a world, we must remember the quiet gladness of the first Easter. This quiet gladness is personal, it is akin to wonder, thanksgiving, reverence – and it is confident. When things are dark and difficult the God of Easter still acts beyond our hoping and gives beyond our asking.

As we watch or read the news we are constantly sickened by sights and first-hand accounts of violence against women and children, against whole groups of people who are labelled and despised. We shall not turn back the tide of such violence by simply employing its own weapons in act or speech. At root the problems are personal: the sickness is in the hearts and minds of men and women. It was to cure this sickness that Christ came and lived and died and rose again.

The enemies of peace, and of reverence for people, their homes and families, the enemies of the beauty and order of the natural world, these enemies have never been more obvious: they are self-centredness and fear. It was these personal enemies with which Christ contended to prove that the love of God which he would share with us can, come what may, never be defeated. We need also to remember *who* these people were to whom this Easter gladness came. They were the people who had reason to feel not only sad about Jesus' death, but also guilty. It was they who had betrayed, deserted and denied him. It is strange that the Gospels should give such prominence to the weakness of the twelve apostles during Jesus' last days, and set their timidity in sharp contrast with the staunchness and fidelity of certain women – for by the time the Gospels were written these men were pillars and princes of the Church.

I think their Easter gladness must have been, at least in part, the gladness of finding themselves *forgiven*. They could convey how much it had meant to be forgiven by making it known how great was their guilt. They were very guilty men, but it was to *them* that Jesus came. He did not abandon them to their shame or distance himself from them. The disciples' gladness lay not simply in the fact that he who was dead was now alive, but also in the fact that he whom they had abandoned did not abandon them. The Easter stories are stories of *reconciliation* – of Jesus coming back even from death to embrace again those who had made themselves strangers. Easter is the Good Shepherd coming back to seek and to save what was lost. The first Easter was not only a demonstration of the power of God in Christ over death: it was also a sign of his faithfulness in seeking and saving the lost, in loving and forgiving the guilty.

It is this same way of forgiveness that the Christian is called to follow. We are to love and forgive our enemies, and pray for our persecutors – however trying that may be. We have seen a fine and impressive example of this quiet Easter faith shining through personal tragedy in a Christian congregation in Ealing.[3] Such heroic healing power could hardly fail to move the most determined cynic.

So Easter is about people being searched out by God's love: it is about being found, healed, restored, forgiven. On the first Easter Sunday no one was confounded, no one was proved to be in the wrong or forced into faith. No one was made an unwilling captive and paraded in the victor's triumph. No one was either cowed or exhilarated by a dramatic display of power. That day was a glad day when the love of God in Christ quietly enfolded again those who had least right to expect it, and so rescued them from the tragedy and darkness they had brought upon themselves.

May this Easter be such a day – a day to remember with quiet gladness the truth at the heart of the Christian gospel, 'that neither death, nor life, nor things present, nor things to come, nor anything else in all creation, will be able to separate us from the love of God in Christ Jesus our Lord.'[4] And so knowing with all our faults and failings that we can never put ourselves out of reach of God's love, there is always a fresh start waiting for each of us – for Christ is risen, the Lord is here, his Spirit is with us.

---

[3] Following a savage attack on a vicarage family.
[4] Romans 8.39.

Ascension

🮰🮰🮰🮰

'Then he led them out as far as Bethany, and lifting up his hands, he blessed them. While he blessed them, he parted from them and was carried up into heaven. And they returned to Jerusalem with great joy, and were continually in the temple blessing God.'[1]

WE ASSOCIATE APOSTOLIC joy more with Easter or Pentecost than the ascension. Yet here it is.[2] In the Lucan account of the ascension, Jesus is parted from the disciples and carried up into heaven. They then return to Jerusalem *with great joy*. We have obviously got it wrong if we think of the ascension as the great farewell. Permanent goodbyes are not usually happy occasions. But the ascension is not the final separation of Jesus from his friends. It is rather the taking up of our humanity into the life of God. All that is beautiful and good in our human life, all that has been suffered or endured in union with Christ, all that has been won in our moral life, all this in Christ is now part of God. So we do well to share the apostles' great joy and to give praise to God.

We have been 'soft pedalling' the ascension for far too long. When I was a young priest, there was a good deal of embarrassment about it. It was all played down or explained away. I remember sermons about Jesus not being a rocket. In retrospect, I think we were guilty of an insufferable form of superiority in assuming that the biblical writers naively believed their three-decker universe to be a scientific description. The ancients understood the dynamics of symbol and image, saga and myth. The Jew who was forbidden to make any kind of visual or tangible image of God would hardly take as literally true and photographically exact those images of God which appeared within his own experience or were reported by others. They were not so foolish as to take poetry to pieces in an attempt to isolate spiritual truth from its fleshly incarnation.

---

[1] Luke 24.50-3.
[2] Sermon at Queen's College, Birmingham, on Ascension Day, 8 May 1986.

We constantly forget that Christianity is a *material* religion. It concerns an historical incarnation, a flesh and blood crucifixion, a bodily resurrection, and it culminates in that taking up of our full humanity into the Godhead which we call the ascension, and which we celebrate in this Eucharist with these earthly creatures of bread and wine. Of course the spirit is also an essential ingredient in our Christianity. But not disembodied spirit, not anti-historical, anti-incarnational and anti-sacramental spiritualism. In this life, we never encounter disembodied spirit and, in the next, we take our experience of flesh and spirit with us. To take less would be to take less than ourselves. The recent fraud case[3] involving claims of witchcraft shows how easily Christians can be misled by a false spiritualism – by a sense of God speaking directly to them of incarnation without the safeguards of the revealed words of Scripture, the historic tradition of the Church and the contemporary experience of the Body of Christ.

In former ages, the symbolism of the ascension spoke clearly enough. In many a medieval roof boss, the ascension is pictured by a group of disciples gazing up at a pair of feet! This replaced an earlier way of representing the ascension as a divine handshake – God's hand extending to help Christ into heaven. That picture of the disciples gazing at a pair of feet we can dismiss as quaint, crude, pre-scientific – but the influence of primitive art on the 20th century (one thinks of Picasso, Jacob Epstein, Henry Moore) ought again to make us cautious about dismissing the power of the primitive. Truths are discerned in the primitive of an elevated kind which the sophisticated are the poorer for dismissing.

Our ancestors knew that the possibility of the human journey to God – ascension – turns for the Christian on the reality of the incarnation. If we jib at the human feet of Christ in heaven, we are showing symptoms of a false spiritualism. The image of the earthly feet or hand in heaven is an important way of stating that to get to God by way of Christ is not to by-pass the physical, the historical and the political but – as von Hügel put it – to keep the closest contact with God's own ways of coming to us. There are no gnostic short cuts. We must go through the finite, the limited, the definite.

Ascension Day completes the great 40 days of Eastertide. In

---

[3] In April 1986 a man claiming to be a satanist was convicted for obtaining by deception over £200,000 from Christians in East Sussex.

the tradition the ascension of Christ is a culminating glimpse of the significance of the resurrection. In today's Matthean gospel, resurrection and ascension are indeed one and the same event. The ascension provides the title deeds of a Christian humanism, based on the fact – as Charles Peguy put it – that 'God too has feared death.' The ascension indicates a way of living by both resurrection and crucifixion at one and the same time. It is easier, of course, to live by the resurrection only, or by the crucifixion only, than by both together. To live by the resurrection only would be to play down all life's jagged edges. We all know Christians for whom life appears to have gone favourably and who display a facile optimism that ignores a suffering humanity. To live by the crucifixion only would be to succumb finally to the view that human life is only and ever tragic. The tragic hero is immensely attractive, but in the end even such heroism can become a histrionic posturing.

The Christian life is neither optimism nor tragedy. To live by both resurrection and crucifixion together, through the action of the Spirit and God, is the meaning of the ascension. So it is only in these, our Christian mysteries, that we can rejoice and mourn at the same time and for the same reason – so says T. S. Eliot's Becket in his Christmas sermon. The medieval roof boss with its human feet in heaven gets it right because those feet forever bear the imprint of the nails of the crucifixion. God has been where we are: he has descended to the depths of human existence, to birth, to suffering and to death itself. But we shall go where God is: with all our human experience of joy and sorrow.

In the end, the glory of the ascended Christ is no different from the glory of the crucified Christ. The glory of God is not the glory with which human power tends both to preserve and advertise itself: it is the moral glory of power expended for the being and well-being of others. This is the glory of the cross. The ascension teaches us that this glory is nothing other than the glory of God. It is before *that* kind of glory that we kneel in homage and wonderful anticipation on Ascension Day: and I do not think that, in the last analysis, any other kind of glory has any right to our homage.

Encountering God: Why I Believe

🞵🞵🞵🞵

WE ARE CONCERNED here[1] to explore some fundamental questions about truth, the existence of God, human destiny, the nature of man – indeed the meaning of life itself. These are fundamental questions, and not to be ignored or dodged. They continue to be asked, despite having been frequently declared meaningless or impossible to answer.

Faith is often the only form of response appropriate to these kinds of ultimate questions. By faith I do not mean an irrational reaction of blind optimism or homespun philosophy displayed by the immature when confronted by complex or trying circumstances: 'It will all turn out for the best, it will all make sense, in the end.' Faith is perhaps more the ability to say 'Yes' to such questions as 'Is there intelligibility, order and purpose in the universe?'

As an undergraduate I well remember Isaiah Berlin telling us it was our duty not to spend our lives lying on a bed of unexamined assumptions. I think one assumption people might be tempted to make is that an archbishop has 'made it' spiritually: he knows what it is all about, he has all the answers.

I would like to examine that assumption. Because I am an archbishop it is obvious that I believe, that I live by faith. But I believe that everybody lives by faith of some kind – only some have articulated and explored their commitment more thoroughly than others. I am here to try to tell you why I believe in God, and find my faith through the Christian way.

Perhaps I should digress just a little and say why, today, I think it is so important that I believe. I was once startled by Bishop Desmond Tutu saying to me, 'I always find it very hard to be a Christian in England, the issues are so blurred: in South Africa everything is so clear-cut.' It does seem to me that audible clashes

---

[1] *Encounters: Exploring Christian Faith* (Darton, Longman and Todd 1986) pp. 3–11. A series of sermons given in Great St Mary's, Cambridge on eight days in February 1986 during an 'ecumenical exploration' of the Christian Faith.

of principle or the oppressions of tyranny can lead to a clearer perception of spiritual values and the meaning of life – look at Poland and how it has responded to the death of the outspoken priest Father Popieluszko.

In Britain we are more inclined to spiritual stagnation: both great sanctity and spectacular wickedness are in short supply. Perhaps we should thank God for the latter. But what of the former? Somehow the Church must be spiritually awakened to hear God's voice speaking through today's events and discoveries – otherwise it will end by speaking only to itself. Some time ago I found myself wondering whether the language used in reporting Terry Waite's operation in Libya (words like 'mission', 'faith' and 'miracle') was merely the residue to a decaying Christianity, or the reflection of an unspoken need for spiritual values to be reasserted.

I believe there *is* an underlying yearning for God and for things spiritual. I shall speak more of this later. I am not (altogether) convinced that it is (or need be) a case of enter progress, exit God; nor that the present-day substitutes for religion (Communism, nationalism, materialism, humanism) will ultimately replace true religion and religious belief. However, we may have to work harder than we do at present to ensure that a sense of religious mystery surrounds our secular humanitarian activities, and that a sense of religious obligation tempers and disciplines our selfishness, if we are to avoid national suicide.

For me it is Christianity which makes sense of more things about the world and about myself than any ideology. But Christianity is not a once for all religion, handed to me on a plate at baptism, completely ready-made, final. One of its greatest strengths is that it does not attempt to explain everything. There is always at its core, as in every relationship, a heart of mystery.

The God who enters into a personal relation with us through Christ is a God of ultimate mystery. We know that saints like John of the Cross and, nearer home, Mother Julian of Norwich, wrestled with these mysteries; there are records of their agonies of mind and heart as their thinking about God was purified in prayer and tested in suffering. They found a faith deeper than would have been possible had they remained superficial and conventional.

Most of us are, at times, like the poet Francis Thompson in 'The Hound of Heaven' – we flee from God when things are hard and the light of faith is flickering. And yet at such times we can say, with the man in the gospels, 'Lord, I believe – help thou my unbelief', trying to make our muted, half-hearted 'Yes' into a fully articulated response that can shape and rule our lives.

These are some of the reasons why I think it is important to believe. But I do not think I have yet approached the question of *why* I believe closely enough. Nor indeed am I sure this is exactly what I am going to do. I think there is a risk in telling or explaining why I believe in God. And the risk is that the God in whom I believe may be obscured or distorted when I state my reasons for believing in him, just as trying to explain why I love a person by describing a particular attribute or talent may imply that they are loved for the attribute or talent rather than for themselves. (So you can tell your girl friend as often as you like *that* you love her, but it's sometimes dangerous to tell her *why* you love her!)

If I say, for instance, that I believe in God because my prayers have sometimes been answered, then I may as well be taken to mean that I believe in the existence of an invisible slot-machine which can sometimes provide me with what I want. And if I say that I believe in God because a friend recovered from cancer when all the doctors had given up hope, I may well seem to be saying that I believe in the existence and effectiveness of an occult healing power.

The God in whom I believe may be, or seem to be, nothing more than my reason for believing in him. I think there are some people of whom this is true: their God simply *is* their reason for believing in him. There is – or was very recently – a well-known American evangelist who regularly appeared on the TV dripping with jewellery, even to the extent of having diamonds set in his teeth! His message was, 'I believe in God, and see how richly he has blessed me. If you believe in him you too will be rich.' The God he preaches is nothing more than the source of riches to those who believe in him.

But I am sure that to most people the God in whom they believe is not simply an answering machine or an occult power-source – just as the person whom they love is not simply a nice voice combined with a talent for dancing and one or two other things. The difficulty is that the more precisely we set out our reasons for believing the more risk we take of suggesting that these reasons for our belief are the actual substance of our belief.

Encountering God: Why I Believe

And here lies the danger of putting forward as our reasons for belief those classical arguments or proofs for the existence of God with which some of you will be familiar. They are claimed – and perhaps justifiably – to be logical demonstrations that, for instance, a First Cause must exist and a most Perfect Being must exist. But if they are our reasons for believing in God, then the God we believe in is (or at least seems to be) no more than a First Cause or a most Perfect Being. Well, I suppose one could believe in a God who was simply that, but it would be a very dim and dull and abstract kind of belief. It would not make much difference to anything, and it would hardly be worth recommending to anybody else. It would be no great achievement to persuade an atheist or agnostic to admit the existence of a First Cause or a Perfect Being.

In making explicit the reasons why we believe in God there is a risk of misleading people about the kind of God we believe in. Just as the safest (and probably most truthful) answer to someone who asks *why* you love him or her is, 'Just because I do, and I can't help it', so the safest, and perhaps the most honest, course for me would be to say, 'Why do I believe in God? . . . Just because I do – and I can't help it', and, having said that, to go on at once to what I believe. But there is rather more to be said.

To go back to this business of loving. I do not apologize for doing so – for believing in God is much more like loving someone than it is like believing there is oil in a certain rock stratum or life on a certain planet. You cannot really say why you love someone, and that all this business about her seductive voice, her shapely figure, fails to express or contain the heart of the matter. But let us suppose someone said: 'You *can't* love Susan. She's no sense of humour at all'; or, 'You shouldn't love Susan. She tells lies.' Well, you might respond with a fist or a kick on the shins, or you might say, 'I know that, but I still love her.' But more likely, especially if the speaker was someone you respected, you would say: 'Susan does have a sense of humour, but it's very subtle and it's not everyone who notices it'; or, 'Susan doesn't tell lies: it's just that she forgets and gets things muddled up.' These words do not give the reason why you love Susan, but they do give the reason why it is not foolish or improper to love her. They do not explain your love – but they do to some degree defend it and justify it.

Similarly I cannot satisfactorily explain why I believe in God, but I can, at least to some extent, defend and justify my belief. I can say, first and with great conviction, that there is *space* for belief in God: huge space, empty space, sensible space, that is almost crying out to be filled.

It is the space of which we are aware when we *wonder at the mystery* of being. By this I do not just mean wonder at the beauty and order of the world, but something more fundamental than that – wonder at the fact that there is anything at all. Wittgenstein wrote in the *Tractatus*, 'The mystical is not *how* the world is but *that* it is', and in a paper on ethics he referred to occasions when he found himself wondering at the existence of the world and saying to himself, 'How remarkable that the world exists, how remarkable that *anything* exists.'[2] We may trace with increasing scientific precision the 'how' of the world, detect evermore exactly the laws and forces which determine its operations and its history, but *that* the world exists, *that* those laws and forces are there, remains a matter for undiminished wonder.

A still greater matter for wonder is my own presence and awareness and consciousness within the world at which I wonder. Here am I, within the mystery, sensing and seeing the mystery, treading on and handling and making use of the mystery – surviving, one might say, by courtesy of the mystery. It cannot be the height of wisdom simply to swim and swan around within the mystery in mindless oblivion. Nor, on the other hand, can it be foolish to have some kind of attitude to the mystery. And to take a certain attitude at this profound level is, I think, certainly the beginning, and possibly even the core and centre, of belief in God. To perceive and respond to the mystery as a *gracious* mystery would be to have an implicit belief in God. So, there is certainly space – intellectual space – for belief in God.

Now comes the second point of my defence. It lies in the special and remarkable character of moral awareness. Kant said there are two things which move mankind to wonder – the starry heavens above and the moral law within. I suppose that by 'wonder at the starry heavens' Kant meant what I have just been thinking of – wonder at the mystery of being. It is when we look up at the night sky and think of its immensity and of our minuteness that the mystery of being is most profoundly experienced.

---

[2] Wittgenstein, L. *Tractatus Logico Philosophicus*. Routledge & Kegan Paul, 1922.

By 'wonder at the moral law within' I think Kant meant what I would describe, rather less imposingly, as 'wonder at the fact that things matter'. The cause for wonder, for vision, is not that things matter to me – subjectively. It is that some things matter objectively, they have a right to matter, and that this is so absolute and irrefutable.

The famine in Ethiopia may or may not matter to me: but there is no doubt that it has a right to matter and that, though I and billions of others may be indifferent, it would still have a right to matter. This right confronts us, and if we ignore it it judges and condemns us. In our awareness the world is not simply registered, as it might be on a spool of film or a tape-recorder. At times it confronts us as mattering; it demands from us some kind of response and condemns us if that response is not forthcoming. There are times when the moral imperative is clear and practical: feeding the hungry, freeing the prisoner, protesting against nuclear weapons or racial discrimination, starting a movement like Amnesty International or Christian Aid.

Moral philosophers may argue as to why – in terms of what general ethical principles – the famine in Ethiopia matters and makes its demands on us, but they can hardly deny that it does so. And so do many other things – public and private, large or small. Our awareness that certain things have a right to matter is as indisputable as our awareness that they exist.

Try telling yourself that it does not matter that you have betrayed a friend, stolen a poor man's coat or, long ago, tortured for your pleasure a helpless cat. Would you buy a second-hand car from a moral philosopher who maintained that these things did not matter? Of course in different ages and societies the moral awareness is sensitive to different things, and in some people it has become atrophied and even, in pathological cases, non-existent. But the conviction that certain things have a right to matter is as widespread among mankind as the conviction that certain things exist.

In the authority with which certain things engage our moral awareness and make their demands there is again *space* – moral space – for belief in God: for the belief that moral demand springs from a source as profoundly mysterious and awesome as does the universe itself.

Let me repeat that I am not stating the reasons why I believe in God: I am simply setting out reasons why it is not foolish to believe – or naive or a mark of senility or wishful thinking. It is with this reminder that I come to the third of these reasons – which is Jesus Christ or, perhaps more exactly, the story of Jesus Christ. This, to put it over-simply, is claimed to be the story of God making himself present, making himself known in and to the world: and in it God is disclosed not as one who exercises a distant and detached supremacy over the world of his creation but as one who, in the greatness of his love for that world, pours out and expends himself 'unto death'.

That story really belongs to the next sermon, but I mention it here for this reason. You may disbelieve the claim made for this story: you may disbelieve the story itself. But I doubt if anyone who seriously attends to the story and the claim made for it can dismiss the whole matter as foolish or trivial or irrelevant – as something of which the truth or falsehood would be immaterial, making no difference to our feeling and attitude about the world in general or our own place in it.

So in and through the story of Jesus Christ and the claims made about it there is again *space* for belief in God. This time I would call it emotional space: if we believe in the God disclosed in the story then there is met the most universal of all human needs – the need to be unconditionally accepted and totally loved.

Here is an illustration. Some time ago I took part in a discussion on transplant operations. A doctor described how that morning after a road accident in Vienna a kidney had been taken from a child's body, frozen, put on a plane, and brought to London where he had put it into another person. 'But', he said, 'I couldn't do this work if I thought that I was simply dealing with a bundle of parts. I don't know how to define life and I'm not very religious, but what I have of faith reminds me that I must respect, no, reverence, every person with whom I have to do.'

It is easy to think of a person as a bundle of parts or a mixture of chemicals – but perhaps that is a case of beginning at the wrong end. See him as the object of God's love, and he comes together as a person. It is easy to see mankind as economic units or racial groups, and it falls apart. See it as the family for whom Christ died and there is emotional fulfilment – a space filled.

So I suppose I cannot say simply *why* I believe in God, but I can point to *space* for such belief – intellectual, moral and emotional space. This at least helps to make sense of Christian belief – belief for which (let me say finally) I remain profoundly grateful. I am thankful for whatever it may be – the example of others, experience of life, the direct touch of God upon me – which has led me to believe and sustained my belief against counter-pressures which are put upon it and against difficulties which are inherent in that belief itself. I do not want to end with pious platitudes about the blessedness of belief, but I have no doubt that if that belief were taken from me I should find the world an intellectual question mark, a moral vacuum and an emotional desert. And those things I firmly do not believe.

Encountering God: What I Believe

PREVIOUSLY I TRIED to say something about *why* I believe – now my theme is *what* I believe.[1] I believe in God through Jesus Christ. That is the heart of the matter. I believe in God as he is disclosed in Jesus Christ – as he meets the world and is met by the world in Jesus Christ. I do not believe that Jesus simply told us what God is like – as I might tell you what someone is like whom I know better. I believe that Jesus *was* what God is like, and that he shows us God rather as an entertainer who plays various roles on television might show me what he is really like by coming in person into my home. Let me put it another way: 'The divine story-teller, the Author of the story of the universe, has done what no novelist could possibly do and entered the story he is telling as one of the characters in it.'[2]

This identity of being between God and Jesus is stated in Christian teaching, but it is not explained. No symbol, analogy or model can carry us any distance, and to my mind all attempts to explain this identity have a tendency only to erode it. I take it as a mystery as far beyond explanation as is the mystery of my own being and of the being of the world. Our safest eloquence is silence.

I believe that Jesus is Emmanuel – God with us, God incarnate, God living a human life. Therefore the story of Jesus is of supreme importance – the story of how he conducted himself and how he fared in the world. We do not know the whole story. All that has ever been reported about Jesus can have occupied no more than a small proportion of his thirty-three years. So there is a mist around the edge of the story. And there is a certain mistiness within the story too. However certain we are about what Jesus said and did in the gospels, we can no longer detect the precise tone of his voice, the ring of his words in the ears of those

---

[1] *Encounters: Exploring Christian Faith.* (Darton, Longman and Todd 1986) pp. 13–20.
[2] Christopher Bryant, *The Heart in Pilgrimage* (Darton, Longman and Todd 1980) p.52.

who heard them, or the significance of his actions in the eyes of those who saw them.

I do not find this mistiness disturbing; and therefore I do not find it disturbing when informed and careful criticism raises doubts about the authenticity of certain incidents in the Gospels, or certain sayings attributed to Jesus. Those doubts simply contribute a little to the general mistiness, and I can accept that uncertainty as I can accept the uncertainty of my memory of my father who died years ago. I have forgotten now much of what my father said and did, and I have discovered that certain things cannot have happened as I remember them. But I am entirely confident that the figure whom I see in my mind is the figure of my father: I still know what kind of man he was, and his particular manner and style, and the shape and quality of his life. So it is with the figure of Jesus.

Let me give you another illustration. When I was Bishop of St Albans there had been before me a bishop called Michael Furse, who was a great character. He had been a bishop exactly forty years before me, and people remembered him vividly. When I went to confirm children, grandparents would often say, 'I was confirmed by Bishop Furse – now he was a *real* bishop!' Sometimes people would tell me what he had said to them: 'What's the use of a banana out of the bunch? It goes bad, doesn't it?' 'The one who endures to the end shall be saved' was one of his favourite texts. I developed a clear picture of Mike Furse, and indeed there came a time when I felt I could almost have written one of his sermons. Sometimes when I was told something about him I would say, 'That can't be true – it doesn't fit in with what I've heard.' I never met him, but the time between us was much the same as the time between the crucifixion and the Gospel writers. Memories are strong enough in our day and they were much stronger in our Lord's. So I am not as sceptical as some about the accuracy of the portrait of Jesus we find in the New Testament.

None the less it does seem particularly appropriate that the figure should emerge from the Gospels with a certain mistiness around it, for within the Gospels Jesus is presented as a distinctly enigmatic figure. He enters without pomp or preparation into the most commonplace scenes of life, yet makes each scene his own. He is casual and unselective, even scandalous in the company he keeps, yet minutely attentive and sensitive to it. His total dedication to God is also easy and intimate. He lives in obedience to the Jewish tradition but presumes to judge it. He is often misunderstood even by those most intimate with him. He wins for himself wonder and admiration, but does not exploit what he has won, and as his fame and following increase he speaks of his rejection, suffering and death. His life poses the persistent, nagging question: 'Who *is* this?' 'Who do men say that I am?' and the manner of his death proposes the answer, 'An offender, a pretender and blasphemer, a misleader of the people'.

Then there followed the insurrection. During the last fifty years, since Professor C H Dodd detected so conclusively the content of the very earliest Christian preaching, it has been difficult to take seriously the account of the origins of Christianity which, up to then, had been widely taught by liberal theologians. They argued that the influence of Jesus's teaching and personality was so powerful in the generation after his death that the belief eventually crystallized that Jesus had actually survived or risen from death.

But that account does not fit the actual historical facts – namely, that the resurrection of Jesus was being preached well before any great attention was being paid by believers to what Jesus had been or had taught in his lifetime. Historically speaking, interest in the life and teaching of Jesus sprang from belief in his resurrection, not vice-versa. It was the resurrection that led to faith, not faith that led to the resurrection. So I cannot assent to any explanation or interpretation of the resurrection which has a tendency to explain it away like this, or deny its roots in history. I doubt in fact whether attempts at explanation of the resurrection are profitable at all. But affirmation is different: from the very beginning it has been the common Christian experience and conviction that Jesus *is* alive, risen from the dead, a present person and a living power.

You may recall that, in connection with the risen Christ, St Paul uses the phrase 'new creation', and the phrase continues to be used in our Christian preaching and theology. If we take it seriously what we are saying is that what happened in the resurrection of Jesus was of the same dimension as what happened in the original, primeval creation – in the creation of the world.

Creation does not submit to the order and regularities of the world: it ordains them. If it is true that in the resurrection of

Jesus new creation appears, then it cannot be explained in terms of the regularities of the old. We must speak of *miracle* – and of miracle in the old-fashioned sense of the word as an unprecedented event which does not fit within, and cannot be explained by, the normalities and regularities of nature.

It may be that we must use the same word, and in the same sense, of certain other events, from the virgin birth onward, recorded in the Gospels and the Acts of the Apostles. One must speak carefully here. Many thoughtful people find that the marvellous order of nature, and the beauties of splendours which appear within that order, are themselves powerful signs of the wisdom and care of God – much more powerful than occasional departures from order. They do not need miracles to show them *that* God is, or *what* God is.

With this point of view I largely agree. But consider this. In the fullness of time, at a particular moment and place within the old creation, God discloses himself. Since God is who he is, that disclosure will be distorted if mankind is bludgeoned or frightened into receiving it: it can be received undistorted only if it is received by faith.

But faith can be born again only if there is first attention – or attention to that particular event or person or place where the disclosure actually is. Remember how in the story of the burning bush Moses is drawn aside by this phenomenon to wait and listen for what may be told him.

> When Moses, musing in the desert, found
> The thorn bush spiking up from the hot ground,
> And saw the branches, on a sudden, bear
> The crackling yellow barberries of fire,
>
> He searched his learning and imagination
> For any logical, neat explanation,
> And turned to go, but turned again and stayed,
> And faced the fire and knew it for his God.[3]

Attention does not compel faith but it precedes faith.

How, I ask myself, was *attention* drawn to Jesus and to the story of Jesus as it was preached in the first generation – attention adequate to the birth of so profound a faith? One certainly cannot exclude the possibility of the miraculous – of events so

---

[3] Norman Nicholson, 'The Burning Bush', from *Five Rivers*. Faber and Faber, 1944.

distinct from the regularities of the old creation that they would draw attention to the particular figure and the particular story through which faith might receive the divine self-disclosure.

This does not necessarily mean that Christians should be expecting or hoping for the miraculous today. For in twenty centuries Jesus and the story of Jesus have become embedded in our culture. We have so many things to draw our attention to that figure and that story, and to suggest that they are worth attending to: things as rich and various as King's College Chapel, Cambridge, the music of Bach and Handel, Michelangelo's Pieta, the example of St Francis and the work of Mother Teresa; the poetry of Blake and Hopkins and Eliot, and the glass of Chartres Cathedral; and a vast range of interpretative writing, from the Gospels themselves to works of our own day. Of these things the first generation of Christians had nothing – nothing at all. It should be no surprise if we do not have the one thing which they had – the attention-drawing power of the miraculous. It does seem to me rather self-indulgent on our part to expect or claim that also.

To return to the resurrection. Those who believed did not immediately assert the identity between Jesus and God: that belief or doctrine emerged through years of continuing experience and reflection. But from the first, believers did (if I may put it like this) mention Jesus and God in the same breath. Jesus had been raised by God, sealed as God's own, exalted to God's right hand. To worship, trust and obey Jesus was to worship, trust and obey God.

We must remember two things. First, the God with whom Jesus is so directly and uniquely associated is no small God, no mere tribal or territorial deity, no member of a pantheon. In Jewish belief of that time God is One, the Almighty creator and Lord of heaven and earth, controller of the destiny of nations.

And the second thing we must remember is that the Jesus who is sealed by this God as his own is the *crucified* One. There is no suggestion that it is only Jesus the teacher or Jesus the healer who is God's own, or that the crucifixion was some kind of exception or violation of that unique relationship in which he stands to God. On the contrary it is Jesus Christ 'and him crucified' whom St Paul preaches, so that we might almost say (and St Paul almost says it) that all that is necessary to know about Jesus is that he was crucified in the flesh and raised by God.

So from the earliest days of Christianity, the creator and Lord of heaven and earth is uniquely associated with the weakness and nakedness of the suffering figure on the cross. I know this is a very inadequate way of stating the matter, but I think it will serve for now. 'The cross', said Luther, 'is the hiding place of the power of God.' And it seems to me that the paradox which this contains is still the great glory and the great difficulty of Christian belief.

I believe, along with all Christians, that God is God, that he is the author and sustainer of a universe infinitely vaster and more complex than our forebears had reason to believe. When I speak of God I must never forget what astronomers are detecting through their radio-telescopes and micro-physicists in their laboratories. I must never reduce or domesticate God to a dimension less awesome than that of the universe itself. I must never confine God within the limits of what satisfies *my* needs, *my* hopes or *my* imagination: on the other hand I believe, with all Christians, that 'God was in Christ reconciling the world to himself', and that the key place or point of reconciliation is the cross. I believe that what we see on the cross is not an interruption of *what* God is or a departure from *where* he is but the central point of a saving and reconciling self-disclosure to the world.

When I speak of God I must never forget the one lost sheep, the one human being in agony or despair; I must never forget the tears of one starving child. I must never sweep such things under the moral carpet; I must never think the world's tragedy is somehow necessary to God's grand design. It is these very things which must be reconciled, these situations which must be healed and saved, if God is truly God of a suffering world. We must never distance God so far from the world that he cannot know within himself its suffering, and cannot be exposed to share its grief. The divine crown is one of thorns.

The world has always been a place of suffering: but now, with wider possibilities of communication, we become ever more aware of the range and dimensions of its suffering. The problem of pain has become, for Christian believers, perhaps *the* problem of our age. I am certain that the problem is not to be met by increasingly unbelievable assertions by Christians that suffering, unacceptable though it is to us, is willed by God and therefore for the best.

I believe that we must assert, by the way we live as well as by what we teach, that suffering is never God's will but always his *burden* – a burden borne by God with no less agony and anguish than when Jesus bore his burden in Gethsemane, or when we must bear our loneliness and despair. 'Only the suffering God can help.'[4] We must assert this; we must assert that God has not left us to drown alone in our own blood, sweat and tears – he too has cried the same tears and sweated the same blood.

At the same time we must assert that he who shares so intimately the world's suffering is also the awesome and most holy author of the world's being, the God of the galaxies, the Alpha and Omega of time and space. Only, I think, if we can affirm both of these things can we make with credibility as well as with conviction the claim which I take to express the very heart of our faith – the claim that 'neither death, nor life, nor angels, nor principalities, nor things present, nor things to come, nor powers, nor height, nor depth, nor anything else in all creation, will be able to separate us from the love of God in Christ Jesus our Lord.'[5]

I want to add an appendix. The life of faith begins with an act of trust. As it goes on the evidence accumulates. We find we are living in God's world, and there are signs all around us of his working, because we have the clue in the Lord of the cross. We often have to renew the act of trust.

The things which happen to us and the things which are demanded of us never compel us to acknowledge they are from God. But gradually our world is reorganized round Christ as its centre, and we have not the proofs we asked for at the beginning but an assurance which is held together by faith and a hope which is stronger than man's proofs.

The Lord of the cross accepted as the word of salvation; that is the core of the matter. It sounds jargon; but it does actually save. It saves from discouragement and despair – all the things that would otherwise discourage you become links that unite you with the Lord on the cross. It commits you to obedience and deals with your disobedience day by day. It saves you in death because death is the last unavoidable thing that unites you with Christ – and beyond it is his resurrection.

---

[4] Bonhoeffer, D. *Letters and Papers from Prison*, ed. E. Bethge, (SCM 1967) p. 361.
[5] Romans 8. 38–9.

There are some people today anxious to speak as if belief were a great burden, and are anxious that no one shall escape without the full load. Let me assure you that the Christians who cope ultimately, I believe, and I have met a good many in the most testing circumstances in a great variety of cultures and countries, are people whose faith is cross and resurrection and not dogged, dull, demanding duty. When they condemn they only condemn the sins that their Lord condemned – hypocrisy, calculated worldliness and offences against the law of love.

I find the emancipated people human beings whose infectious faith seems not unbelievable but unquenchable. I want to belong to this company.

Doctrine

I WELCOME THIS debate[1] and congratulate the Bishop of Winchester[2] on his opening speech. I hope that the House of Bishops will return to the Synod with reflections worthy of the high standard he has set, and will only regret that by that time he will no longer be one of our number.

The Church of God has a gospel to proclaim, a faith to affirm. Even though the entire course of Church history has been marked by controversies on issues great and small, the Church is still not a debating society but the people of God, called to witness boldly to his goodness in creation, to his inestimable love in redemption.

To be a Christian is to worship and obey Jesus as Lord. Our historic conviction is that in Christ the creator himself brought to our ravaged humanity a way of healing and salvation. We believe that Jesus Christ is a model to all humanity in his faithfulness to his calling and in embodying the very love of God. Equally we believe that he is more than we are. We see not only humanity as God intended it to be but the very presence of God, in one who uniquely revealed the Father and mediates to us his love and grace, the forgiveness of our sins, the recreation of our true humanity, and eternal life. What we say about the birth, life, death and resurrection of our Lord finds its ground in the witness of the apostles and in the experience of all the people of God. But *our* resurrection depends upon his. To speak of the risen Lord is to speak of something that happened to Jesus Christ not merely of something that happened to his disciples.

I think it right to begin in this way. It expands a short earlier statement that the doctrines of the incarnation and resurrection are not in doubt among your bishops. The issues about the limits of interpreting credal statements which have concerned us in recent months are far from new. A nerve has been touched and exposed with painful effect, but not for the first time. Uncertainty

---

[1] Speech in the General Synod on 13 February 1985 during the debate on doctrine.
[2] The Rt Rev. John Vernon Taylor.

about matters of belief and insecurity about authority – these are nerves never far from the surface in a Church which takes pride in its breadth, its tolerance, its liberty and in T.S. Eliot's phrase its 'continence in affirmation'.

Recent controversy has touched not only the central nervous system of our Anglican ethos. It has touched too the mood of the moment. The sixties and seventies were times when we learnt to live with questions and uncertainty; years when every inherited value and confidence seemed fit to be challenged and consigned to the crucible of criticism. In the eighties the questions are still with us but now there is impatience for answers.

Interest and enquiry about the Christian faith go hand-in-hand with uncertainty about the Church's ability and authority to provide the answers. That is why, for example, I said in 1981 that: 'There is an urgent need for statements on particular theological and ethical problems written in a way and in a compass attractive to the synodsman or woman, the PCC member, the leader of the youth group, the organizer of the intercession circle.' This was a plea for a shift in emphasis in the future work of our Doctrine Commission. That Commission has a special relationship to the bishops and in the short time available this morning I would like to say something about the responsibilities of the bishop on two counts:

First the bishop is the guardian of the tradition. From the earliest times the bishop's essential, defining role has been that of teacher and expounder of God's word. The bishop's *cathedra* is a teaching chair, not a royal throne. Our canon says of diocesan bishops: 'It appertains to his office to teach and to uphold sound and wholesome doctrine, and to banish and drive away all erroneous and strange opinions.' In the service of consecration the archbishop declares the bishop's 'special responsiblity to maintain and further the unity of the Church, to uphold its discipline and to guard its faith'.

A bishop's consecration imposes a certain conservative responsibility. He is a guarantee of historic continuity. He is a steward of the apostolic faith which is our common Christian heritage. He will, of course, take advice from theologians and others, but if he is to be true to his vocation the bishop must regard himself as pre-eminently the trustee of tradition in his diocese and with his fellow bishops in the Church at large. There may be other calls to keep him in what Archbishop Tait called 'a perpetual state of perspiration', but, if they deflect him from his main responsibility of representing the faith of the Church to the world, they must be resisted.

Secondly the bishop is the interpreter of the tradition. He is a representative figure. Standing within the Church, he represents the Church to the Church. He shares its life and thought and actions. This means he embodies not only the Church's apostolic authority but also the faith, doubts, perplexities and aspirations of every Christian. The bishop is no more exempt from the need to examine, test and explore the truth of his faith than any Christian, ordained or lay. The bishop is not an automaton but a man of flesh and blood, a man of doubt as well as faith, a man seeking and finding, a man as far from the clear certainties of the celestial city as the rest of the pilgrim church. Talk of the bishop's conservative responsibility, of his guardianship of the tradition, can sound as though what is meant by tradition and the apostolic faith is something pre-packed and deep-frozen; something essentially static and unchanging; something handed down, complete and intact, from one generation to the next. Such a view neglects the limits of human expression and is contrary to the Anglican spirit of intellectual freedom and independence.

The tradition stands, of course, and it commands authority, but in Anglicanism it is an authority of *sources* for dogma as much as of dogma itself. 'The doctrine of the Church of England is grounded in the Holy Scriptures and in such teachings of the ancient fathers and councils of the Church as are agreeable to the said Scriptures.' The historic formulas of our Church are the deposits at a particular moment of the same stream of tradition, but they remain profoundly important as guidelines and boundaries for the Church's thinking. They embody the accumulated wisdom of the Church's past in defining the limits of fruitful enquiry. But they do not preclude such enquiry. On the contrary, they are a stimulus to renewed attempts to interpret belief and its historic roots in ways which intellectually, personally and pastorally satisfy: 'We do not reverence tradition by wrapping it in a napkin and burying it in our garden, reflecting that in due course we will be able to produce it intact again. We reverence tradition by using it.' So writes John McManners.[3]

---

[3] Regius Professor of Ecclesiastical History, Oxford University, in his chapter 'The Individual in the Church of England' in the Doctrine Commission's book *Believing in the Church* (SPCK 1981) p. 224.

A vigorous Church needs leadership which is a mixture of conservative and radical, heir and critic. We need shepherds not only to repel wolves from the fold, but also to lead the flock to new and more fertile pastures. The bishop is responsible for both preservation and constant renewal of the faith. If he is to be true to his ancient title of *pontifex*, the bishop must be a bridge-builder, who, in his own thinking and teaching, attempts to bestride the narrow worlds of mindless dogmatism on the one hand and rootless individualism on the other. Earthed firmly in the tradition and inspired by the Spirit, he coaxes, guides and encourages others in the common task of fresh exploration and application of that tradition and its historic content. These are the marks of true guardianship.

Clearly such a path is fraught with difficulty and danger and it is a wise bishop who treads there with care and reverence. Bishop John Robinson, no stranger to this perilous path, had this prudent and prophetic counsel to give:

> a bishop will be the more aware that his lightest word is liable to be taken up – and distorted – by the public media. The inordinate attention paid to what he says derives almost entirely from his office, and his utterances and actions will therefore appear, particularly outside the Church, but also to embarrassed faithful within, to commit many others than himself. This means that he must exercise special prudence and imagination. . . . And he will have the theological responsibility, not only of being as well read and well informed as his time and capacity allow, but of being careful to insist when he is speaking with the authority of his office and when he is not. But in the last analysis, the responsibility of the bishop in doctrine is different only in degree, not in kind, from that of any other baptised Christian. The Church must give positive witness to the fact that integrity is a more fundamental theological virtue than orthodoxy. . . . A man of unimpeachable orthodoxy but uncertain integrity is a far greater threat to Christian truth than the man of questionable orthodoxy but undeniable integrity[4]

I should like to end with some reflections on the Church itself. First, Churches do change; the most unchanging of Churches change. Churches are habitually engaged in correcting their own

---

[4] 'Prophetic Ministry in the World', a submission for the Report of the Advisory Committee of the Episcopal Church of the USA: Bayne, S. F. jnr., ed. *Theological Freedom and Social Responsibility*. (New York, Seabury Press 1967) pp. 142, 144. Reprinted in *Christian Freedom in a Permissive Society* (SCM Press 1970) pp. 123–9.

past; but such change is done by emendation, by development, by re-emphasis, and not by repudiation.

Secondly, a Church needs authority; it cannot do without it. But if it became as tidy as the High Courts of Justice we should suspect it. The Church is not like a schoolteacher who must expel a boy from school lest he influence the others to wickedness. It is not like a king who must expel a troublesome subject. It is more like a mother with children, holding a lively family together. A Church cannot do without authority, but it ought to be gentle, tranquil, long-suffering and therefore sometimes untidy. All ministerial authority is subject to the word of God and the Spirit who blows where it will.

Thirdly when disputes arise we must remember the teaching of St Paul that everyone who receives through the Spirit a function in the body and the gift or capacity to perform it should so express the function that the body as a whole, including its weaker members, is held together, built up and edified.[5]

I hope that the bishops will listen to this debate in such a way that they are able to fulfil their office for the building up of the body – the more effectively to proclaim the Gospel and to affirm the faith which I tried to express at the start of my speech.

---

[5] See Ephesians 4.7, 15–16.

Religion and Humanity

ONE OF THE cherished privileges of an Archbishop of Canterbury is his association with All Souls.[1] A framed copy of the Founder's Prayer holds pride of place outside my chapel at Lambeth Palace – a daily reminder to an often hard-pressed archbishop of the abiding virtues of godliness and good learning. My visits here signal far more than dutiful obedience to statute or tradition.

It seems that in this (at least) a modern archbishop differs from his forebears. The archives of All Souls have a long series of letters between the college and the visitor and they are a remarkable study in archiepiscopal exasperation. The view from Lambeth, at least down to the 19th century, was that the college was a decidedly frivolous place and needed to be brought back to a proper religious and academic seriousness. In 1709 Archbishop Tenison was much angered to learn that four discontented fellows of the younger sort had made the Warden's life a misery by having Morris dancers jump up and down in the room next to his bedroom. 'What has happened to Religion and Humanity?' he demanded.

'What has happened to Religion and Humanity?' – let this serve as my theme for this commemoration sermon. For Tenison it seemed only natural that the two should go together – in this he was giving voice to a long tradition of Christian humanism. The Fathers of the Early Church had sought to show the compatibility of classical learning and Christian teaching – indeed they forged the fundamental doctrines of the Christian creeds out of the concepts and categories of Greek philosophy. In this same tradition Christian artists of the Renaissance and theologians of the Reformation like Erasmus sought to recommend faith in Jesus Christ as the key to a true understanding of the value and possibilities of our humanity.

There have been, of course, Christians who have sought to

---

[1] Sermon preached at a service of Commemoration at All Souls' College, Oxford on Sunday 3 November 1985.

contrast the divine and the human, who have set out a view of religion so other-worldly that human reason and human achievements and relationships have been seen as little worth beside the immense weight of divine glory. Edward Gibbon castigated such a Christianity as an enemy to human happiness and usefulness. It was not in *this* world he wrote, 'that the primitive Christians were desirous of making themselves either agreeable or useful'. The sadness is that he seems to have thought that this was the only Christianity there was.

And naturally there have been humanists who have sought to give an account of man entirely in terms of himself. This too leaves many questions unanswered about the nature and end of our humanity, and it seems to lead on to attitudes strangely cynical, even inhumane. The man who denies the facts of God and the heavenly realms foreshortens the perspective of human life. Inevitably he conducts his life on a short-term policy. Those powers and qualities that can be developed most quickly are those which he nourishes, and the needs which proceed from them are those which he seeks to satisfy. For patience and the things that call for patience there is little place or time. It is an unhappy type of humanity that an earth-bound Utopianism produces – and a terrible fact that when men will have nothing of the heavenly city they cannot build a tolerable society on earth.

Perhaps in every generation there is need for a traditional Christian assertion of belief both in God and humanity: our faith that man is a divine creation and that in Christ is to be found the true dimension and the real nobility of purpose and possibilities of our humankind.

There is one sense in which Christians and humanists nowadays find themselves very close in their attitudes. Both have a growing realization that in our modern world humanity is one: that there is a single condition of being human, and it is this which is more significant than all the different groups and categories into which human beings are usually divided – whether by race or sex, between the civilized and the uncivilized, between the law-abiding and the criminal, even between the faithful and the unfaithful, the saved and the lost.

We feel increasingly that these distinctions are often either trivial or arbitrary and that the making of them is presumptuous. In the area of morals we assert more emphatically that the social duty and respect which is owed to *any* is owed to *all*. And in the religious field we become more convinced that if God is merciful the range of his mercy will not be bounded by our distinctions. If he is merciful to *any* he will be merciful to *all*. The approach is different but each stands with the other in opposition to the view that *some* members of the human family matter less than others and that there are some categories, the abnormal, the criminal, the less developed, which may be taken to count for little. Such practical agreement is the basis for vitally necessary common action in a world which knows much want, injustice and inhumanity.

Now, though, both Christians and humanists are faced with a new and urgent problem – namely, that both in theory and practice the boundaries of the human family are becoming unclear. Practical problems are arising, especially in the medical field: whether, for instance, a human foetus at a certain stage of development may be destroyed or used for experiment, or whether that foetus has all the rights and value of a human being; whether the elderly victim of severe brain damage should or should not be sustained indefinitely in some kind of minimal life by sophisticated medical support. And behind these practical dilemmas there lies the theoretical difficulty of defining what it is that decisively distinguishes the human from the non-human – a difficulty that increases as, for instance, naturalists detect in non-human creatures subtleties of behaviour and complexities of communication which, until recently, would have been thought uniquely and exclusively human.

With the further progress of science such dilemmas and difficulties will certainly increase. As they do, I think that thoughtful opinion will become polarized: there will be two distinct and opposite kinds of response to the problem. One will be to maintain the present status and value of the human by defining in very clear and unambiguous terms the boundary between the human and the non-human. I am sure that it would be very difficult to produce such a definition for it would presumably have to include such complex terms as 'rationality', 'self-awareness' and 'moral sense'.

To achieve a wide measure of agreement on a definition of the human would obviously be difficult: but, supposing it could be done, then a clear boundary would be fixed, and one would be able to say that all that lay outside it was available and expendable for the benefit – in the broadest sense – of all that lay inside.

So, to achieve, or at least to search for, a widely acceptable definition of the human would be one response to the problems which face us. The other and opposite response would be to maintain the status and value of the human by raising or enhancing the value of the non-human. The question of the definition of the human would then be less important: for intrinsic value, varying in degree but on the same *scale* of value, would be seen to extend far beyond the boundary fixed by *any* definition of the human. Beyond the indefinite edge of the human would lie a world of creatures and things valuable on their own account and not simply for the support or interest or delight which they provided for the human. The value of, let us say, a horse would not lie simply in its capacity to give service or delight to man. It would have its own intrinsic value. No doubt that value would be less than the intrinsic value of a man – and so one might properly destroy a horse to save a human life. But the intrinsic value of the horse would not be negligible – so that it would not be proper to destroy an indefinite number of horses to save or prolong one human life or to confer some marginal benefit on a number of human lives. The values of nature and of man would be seen to belong on the same *scale* of value: and nature would no longer be regarded as indefinitely available and expendable for the benefit of man.

I both hope and believe that it is this second response that Christianity will make to the problems which we are considering – that it will maintain the value, the preciousness, of the human by preaching with great emphasis the preciousness of the non-human also – of all that is. For the Christian concept of God forbids the idea of a *cheap creation*, of a throwaway universe in which everything is in principle expendable save human existence. For the Christian, the *whole* universe is a work of love – all is interrelated in God's creating and ever-renewing love. Nothing which is made in love is cheap. The value, the worth of natural things is not found in man's view of himself and his needs, but in the goodness of God who made all things good and precious in his sight.

Such a view finds support in certain rather neglected areas of the Christian tradition. One of the great mystics of Eastern Christendom, Isaac of Syria – a large quantity of whose unpublished and unknown works of the 8th century were recently discovered in a Bodleian manuscript – speaks in memorable terms of the all-embracing concern of the one whose heart is full of the love of God:

> What is a charitable heart? [he asks] It is a heart which is burning with love for the whole creation, for men, for the birds, for the beasts, for the demons – for all creatures. He who has such a heart cannot bear to see or learn from others of any suffering, even the smallest pain, being inflicted on any creature.

Very different is the attitude reflected in the account by John Aubrey, the 17th century antiquary, of a Lord Mayor's show in which the theme was 'Creation'. The passing tableaux and painted scenes represented various aspects of the creation but over each a large placard proclaimed: 'And all for man!' I doubt whether such a self-centred Christian humanism would find much favour or acceptance nowadays. As a recent Christian writer has said: 'An exclusive preoccupation with *human* well-being is beginning to seem distinctly *parochial*.' It will seem even more parochial as we learn more and more about the complex threads which bind our human capacity for rationality and self awareness to the physiological and physical infrastructure in which all life and all being share.

I do not know how humanism will respond to the problems and dilemmas which confront us today. If it does so by drawing boundaries around the human and locating all value within them, then I think that humanism and Christianity will tend once again to move apart. For I cannot think that Christians will be content to believe in a God who made without care or love the mysterious powers and splendours of the primeval world, and who began to love only when human beings appeared.

The Scriptures tell of a God who 'covers the earth with the deep like as with a garment'; who 'waters the hills from above' and 'plants the cedars of Libanus'; who 'opens his hand' to feed the beasts of the wild no less than the children of men, and with his own breathing gives life to all that lives. With such intimate care and wisdom, says the Psalmist, were the earth and the world made – and a care so close and intimate as this can hardly be anything less than love.

For the Christian, the love of God must embrace far more than the human family. That divine love must so enfold the universe itself that nothing within it may be thought of as cheap or expendable, and, furthermore, that nothing, 'neither death, nor life, nor angels, nor principalities, nor powers, nor things present, nor things to come, nor height, nor depth, nor any other creature, shall be able to separate us from the love of God in Christ Jesus Our Lord'[2] – to whom with the Father and the Holy Ghost, be all honour and praise, now and for evermore. Amen.

---

[2] Romans 8.38–9.

The Nature of Christian Belief

🖪🖪🖪🖪

NOT FOR A long time have the bishops corporately spent so many hours in theological reflection as in these last two years.[1] That in itself has been real gain. And, if the Church will allow them to do so, the bishops intend to keep theology at the centre of their concerns.

Preparatory study for the Bishops' Report on 'The Nature of Christian Belief' began in earnest at Manchester in the summer of last year. There, with adversarial attitudes laid aside, we conferred together as brother bishops seeking the right words to state the common faith which holds us together. The basic material for our report came from that meeting, and subsequent modifications have been scrutinized and revised at every stage by the House of Bishops in full session. The result is a consensus document. Some would want to alter this point, some that, but the result comes from us all. It is our best attempt, without ambiguity and without concealing disagreement, to state where we stand on the issues put to us by Synod. I believe we have produced a document which stands in a fine tradition. 'What is notable in Anglican history', wrote Stephen Neill,[2] 'is not that violent passions have sometimes been stirred up, but that in times of passion, the climate of equable and discriminating study has so soon been restored.'

There is indeed nothing new about doctrinal conflict in the Church. It has ever been so and, despite its discomfort and pain, such controversy is a sign of Christian vitality and vigour. We only debate what we care about. The House of Bishops has not tried to dampen conflict, but to ensure that, instead of becoming a source of division and discontent, it should prove instead the creative clash which generates sparks of fresh insight and fresh commitment.

We recognize, with the ARCIC report on Authority, that

---

[1] Speech to the General Synod held at York on 6 July 1986.
[2] 1900–84: Bishop of Tinevelli, South India.

when conflict 'endangers unity or threatens to distort the gospel the Church must have effective means for resolving it'. Some have thought that the Church of England has no such means, that it can be nothing more than a debating society or umbrella under which individuals shelter to forge a faith of their own. The House of Bishops makes it clear that this is not so. At every baptism the faith of the creeds is proclaimed: 'This is the faith of the Church – this is our faith. We believe and trust in one God, Father, Son, and Holy Spirit'. The bishops' Statement makes plain that the Church of England remains loyal to its adherence to the apostolic faith, 'uniquely revealed in the holy Scriptures and set forth in the catholic creeds, and to which its official formularies bear witness'.

Of course, we realize that no verbal propositions, however sacrosanct, are ever adequate to express the majesty and mystery of God. As St Hilary, one of Athanasius' supporters wrote: 'We are compelled to attempt what is unattainable, to climb where we cannot reach, to speak what we cannot utter. Instead of the bare adoration of faith we are compelled to entrust the deep things of religion to the perils of human expression.' But, we realize too that words are fashioned to provide a springboard to propel us into personal response to the truth and love of God. We believe words are signposts we can trust – words through which we can receive the very Word of God.

In affirming our common faith, the bishops do not stand alone or aloof as the 'teaching Church' addressing the 'learning Church'. We are engaged in a common task. Our mission to proclaim and to safeguard the Gospel involves the whole people of God. It is perfectly right and proper that the Statement of the House of Bishops should be the subject of discussion and debate in this Synod. In this way we give expression to our conviction that all are disciples, and all are anointed with the spirit of truth. Yet the bishops in Synod have not lost their special collegial responsibility for preserving truth and discerning error, for maintaining the unity of the Church, and upholding its discipline and guarding its faith. Perhaps we are best seen as a collective conductor, trying to weld a sometimes discordant set of musicians into an orchestra, inducing virtuoso soloists to bring their gifts to the common enterprise: at one minute quietening the blaring brass, the next drawing out the reticent wind section. And all so that, in the words of St Ignatius of Antioch, 'By your concord and harmonious love Jesus Christ may be sung'. Our statement shows us engaged in such work. It has not been easy. We cannot pretend all was sweetness and light. The Statement has been called dull and unexciting. Perhaps our corporate style is too ponderous to convey adventure and enthusiasm; but it beats in our breasts nevertheless. The excitement comes when, through these inadequate words, we hear afresh the Word of God, and struggle to respond.

Excitement, yes, but also difficulties. 'When God gave us his Son who is his one Word', wrote St John of the Cross, 'he spoke everything to us, once and for all in that one Word. There is nothing further for him to say.' And yet there *is* something further for *us* to say. The incarnate God has committed himself to the course of history. His gospel passes through different cultures and changing times. There is real development in our understanding of God's gift in Christ. Today's affirmation of the faith revealed in Scripture and creed cannot be a simple repetition. It must take account of fresh insights as well as new problems. We shall do disservice to the Christian cause if we presuppose that there is nothing serious to discuss and analyse, and if we talk as if the degree to which a theological teacher denies the existence of a problem is the measure of his or her loyalty to the Church. The questions before us are being asked – and not just by people outside the community of faith. The questions are in the minds of all men and women of the twentieth century educated to understand how contemporary historians and scientists discover and judge the truth.

Our particular difficulty is in the relationship of faith to history. We are united in believing that our Christian faith is built on an irreducible core of historical events – in essence, that Jesus lived, died and rose again. The Report is clear that 'Historical fact does matter'.[3] There cannot be authentic Christian faith without historical event. There must be enough fact to sustain faith. We are united too in recognizing that the meaning of these events is frequently expressed in the language of legend, poetry and metaphor – such as the descent and ascent of the Son of God. Like the gospels themselves, our creed is a multi-dimensional picture in which symbol and event are so blended together as to express the image of the invisible God.

[3] para. 22.

This fundamentally visual nature of our faith, this call to behold the glory, should not be forgotten. Before ever human beings wrote and read, they painted and looked at pictures. Of course, the art critic's duty is to analyse the picture, to reason, talk and write about it. As critic, he will point out that it is not always clear which parts of the portrait are events and which parts symbol. Faced with the stories of the virginal conception or the empty tomb, he will ask into which category they should be fitted. While the bishops confidently reaffirm the Church's portrait of Christ, we recognize honest difficulties in this delicate borderline between event and symbol, historical fact and interpretation. In our Report, we have not pretended to agreement on specific points where such agreement does not exist. We think it right to be frank about these difficulties, even if it does leave a less tidy image of our Church than some would desire. That the vast majority of Christians throughout history have accepted the empty tomb and the virginal conception as historical facts is not in dispute. Any other interpretation is a departure from that held in the universal Church. For this majority such facts sustain and illumine faith in the resurrection and incarnation. But they are by no means the only facts on which those great central beliefs rest. That is why it is possible to believe fully in the resurrection and incarnation while reserving judgement on these specific historical points.

Faith does not centre on negations – the absence of a human father or the emptiness of a tomb. The mainstream of the Church believes that these negations are entailed by its affirmations, but they cannot be said to be the heart of the matter. It is the action of God not the passivity of Joseph which is central. It is Christ risen in the completeness of his glorified humanity not the vacating of a tomb which is central.

'Truth', said Newman, 'is wrought out by many minds working freely together.' Yes, *freely* together. It is the conviction of the Church of England that individuals grow in faith. We are confident that the Church is enriched when our feet are set on a path broad enough for us to move forward with freedom and integrity. We need to respect one another's right to occupy such a path. We need to be patient and sensitive with one another's difficulties. We grow in freedom. When the old common language of Christendom is strained to breaking point, and words and images have to be hammered anew to perform their ancient task, we must not be too quick on the draw in gunning down what seems to be heresy.

But explorers will only receive the patient attention they deserve when they refuse to be lone pioneers, and declare their solidarity with the household of faith; when they have not only voices eager to speak, but ears close enough to the ground to catch and cultivate the shy murmurings of the people of God.

The bishops have not written this Report expecting to please everyone. Those who see in every critical enquiry a threat to faith are sure to dislike it. So too will radical liberals if they hold in contempt the tradition of the Church, or think theology a barren cloudland.

The Synod asked us what we believe: in this document we have told you. We have also given reasoned discussion of the central credenda. We have not thought it our duty to construct a barbed wire entanglement to keep anybody out, but have sought to affirm the articles of faith – without reservation, and without excluding exploration.

Sometimes people suggest or hint that there can be a double standard of truth – one for professors and academic teachers of theology, another for the Church's officers and accredited teachers. I confess that I am very ill at ease with this suggestion. Obviously academics in search of new things to say may occasionally yield to the temptation to propose new ideas that lack any sufficient historical basis. We may safely leave the critical demolition of mere novelties and extravagances to other academics. Bishops have other things to see to. They have, however, the duty, perhaps, to ask Christian teachers, as they exercise their rights of freedom and unfettered enquiry, to be considerate in expression, prudent in presentation, and resistant to the mere itch of rashness. They will know as we do that few are helped to think through a problem if their minds are subjected to violent shocks.

Belief is not a purely individual thing. Each believer needs a supportive and strengthening community of faith and worship to which to belong. That is why a Church in which 'anything goes' will inevitably fragment. If individuals are to be free for their own adventure of exploration into God, they actually will do that best from within a community with structure, shape and commitment, rooted firmly in tradition. Anglicanism lives dangerously because it tries to maximize that liberty for the individual without losing the central definition and coherence of belief and practice. This is the spirit in which the House has responded to this Synod, and we hope to have your critical solidarity in our effort to offer guidance to our Church in these things.

Concern for the Spiritual

🔳🔳🔳🔳

It is death to limit oneself to what is unspiritual; life and peace can only come with concern for the spiritual.[1]

THE LAST TIME I stood in the Minster I did so among all the dirt and desolation of fire. The roof lay open to the sky, charred timbers were piled high where they had fallen, the floor was awash with blackened water. Now, two years later,[2] after much courageous and determined effort, and not a little theological insinuation, the Minster once again lifts our hearts to things spiritual. And we need it. A wise friend with some of the melancholy of old age said to me: 'As a nation we are afflicted with conceit – showing off our past, like our cathedrals, without cherishing the qualities that produced them. We are afflicted by sourness in our confrontations and quarrels. We are afflicted by timidity about the future.'

Conceit, sourness and timidity. Can the Church not follow a more excellent way? And that happens to be the theme for this Sunday. It is derived from the beautiful Gelasian collect for the day: 'Pour into our hearts that most excellent gift of love, the true bond of peace and of all virtues, without which whoever lives is counted dead before you.' What better theme could we have in the midst of a General Synod that may test to the utmost our capacity for Christian love? 'The more excellent way': the heart of our gospel and calling.

Originally that collect was not attached specifically to this Sunday. It stood first in a collection of sixteen collects that were headed 'For Sundays', suggesting that, once Pentecost was past, the Church was free to turn its attention and devotion to any aspect of Christian life the preacher might choose. These are some verses by J M Falkner:

[1] Romans 8.6.
[2] Sermon preached in York Minster on 6 July 1986 at the Eucharist attended by the General Synod.

> We have done with dogma and divinity
>   Easter and Whitsun past,
> The long, long Sundays after Trinity
>   Are with us at last;
> The passionless Sundays after Trinity,
>   Neither feast day nor fast.
>
> Christmas comes with plenty,
>   Lent spreads out its pall,
> But these are five and twenty,
>   The longest Sundays of all;
> The placid Sundays after Trinity,
>   Wheat-harvest, Fruit-harvest, Fall.[3]

There is a true rhythm in that division of our annual cycle. Half a year to tell and retell the events of salvation from Advent to Pentecost: half a year to work that salvation deeper into daily living. In that scheme we can never be done with doctrine and divinity. Whatever aspect of life we choose to contemplate in the second half of the cycle, it must always refer back to the paramount act of God in Christ, and its implications for Christian life. Stick to the telling of that story, and wisdom for every other concern or controversy will be added to you. This is what it means to be spiritually minded – so to dwell upon the inexhaustible meaning of the incarnation, death and resurrection of Jesus and the gift of the Spirit that every other issue is seen in the light of it.

Set in that light, 'Wheat-harvest, Fruit-harvest, Fall' are all pregnant with fresh significance. Discourse upon them never so brilliantly *without* that reference, and you may as well talk of 'ships and shoes and sealing wax, of cabbages and kings'. Sunday sermons and Synod debates sound much like any other disputatious chat show so long as we 'limit ourselves to what is unspiritual'; so long as we think and talk like anyone else without that transforming reference to the great simplicities at the heart of the Gospel. 'Life and peace can only come with concern for the spiritual.'

'Life and peace' is not quite the same thing as having a peaceful life. I wish it were. The peace of Christ is not the removal of conflict but the containing of conflict in a deeper unity. St Paul

---

[3] From Larkin, P., ed., *The Oxford Book of Twentieth-Century English Verse* (Oxford University Press 1978) p. 40.

believed that it happens when the divisive issues are brought into the light of the great simplicities of the gospel.

> I have been told, my brothers, that there are quarrels among you. What I mean is this: each of you is saying, 'I am Paul's man', or 'I am for Apollos', 'I follow Cephas', or (and here is the greatest arrogance of all) 'I am Christ's'. Surely Christ has not been divided among you! Was it Paul who was crucified for you? Was it in the name of Paul that you were baptized?[4]

Notice he does not ask 'Was Paul given the primacy?', or 'Was Apollos one of the Twelve?' These would have been easy and attractive ploys to a carnal mind, and would have fuelled the discord nicely. Paul recalled them only to fundamentals – to Christ's death, and our baptism into it. For, as he writes later, 'Can you not see that while there is strife and jealousy among you, you are living on the purely human level of the unspiritual mind?'

The risk of those early Gentile churches dividing and decaying must have been considerable. They had no ancient cathedrals to symbolize their traditions. One new sect was as good as another for those with an itch for self-assertion or security. There was nothing to hold them together except the essentials of the Gospel. Their mutual love had to depend on a loyalty to those essential truths which overrode every point of conflict.

But, 'As lawlessness spreads,' said Jesus, 'men's love for one another will grow cold'. That word lawlessness, *anomia*, ought not to be read as a general synonym for wickedness. Rather, it denotes a particular destructive impatience which is much in evidence in our society. One of the leading sociologists of our time, Professor Robert Merton of Columbia University, applies this word, *anomia*, to those who, unable to tolerate more than a limited degree of frustration, are prepared to flout the conventions of their community, and even to destroy it, rather than see it take a direction to which they are opposed. Against this prevalent malaise the Church of Jesus Christ should set its more excellent way of handling conflict. St Paul did not ask deeply divided Christians to surrender their convictions. He asked them to accept one another as Christ had accepted them. There is no reason for us to suppose that the questions which split the Church then – Sunday observance in a pagan society, the use of

---

[4] Corinthians 1.11–13.

foods implicated in pagan ritual – were of any less moment than our controversies are to us.

Everyone, says St Paul, should have reached conviction in his own mind . . . If you have a clear conviction, apply it to yourself in the sight of God. That is the first guideline. The next is: Cease judging one another. We may disagree profoundly and argue passionately, but the tarbrush is not part of the Christian armoury. The third guideline is that no obstacle or stumbling block be placed in a brother's or sister's way. Each of us should accept as our own burden the tender scruples of weaker Christians and not consider ourselves. That is as far as St Paul will go. He never suggests that the whole Church should eat the questionable food or forgo it. Neither the robust conscience nor the tender scruple is to be made absolute. Those who eat and those who abstain, those who keep Sunday and those who regard all days alike – all must accept one another as Christ has accepted them. That is the true nature of the Church and we need it so for our salvation.

This is the festival day of St Thomas More, a martyr for steadfast conviction if ever there was one. He wrote his *Utopia*[5] as a speculative essay on the best possible form of government, but because of the perilous regime under which he lived, he cast his ideas in the form of a narrative of discovery. In the 'nowhere island' of Utopia he found great religious toleration, but no religious indifference. Particularly exacting standards were demanded of their priests – who, incidentally, included women, though widowed and old. It was the king, Utopus, who introduced this tolerance since he had formerly conquered the island by reason of the religious dissension among its inhabitants. Says Thomas More:

> Though there be one religion which alone is true, and all other vain and superstitious, yet did the king well foresee that the truth of the one power would at the last issue out and come to light. But if contention and debate in that behalf should continually be used, as the worst men be most obstinate and stubborn, he perceived that then the best and holiest religion would be trodden underfoot and destroyed by most vain superstitions, even as good corn is by thorns and weeds overgrown and choked.

Words of wisdom and warning to remember in the days before

---
[5] First published 1516.

us – when patience will be provoked, sympathy strained, and tolerance tried. Let us not forget God's more excellent way of love – to confound our conceits, to sweeten our sorrows, and to banish our timidity. For 'It is death to limit oneself to what is unspiritual; life and peace can only come with concern for the spiritual'. Amen.

LIGHT – FOR THE NATION

Zeebrugge Ferry Disaster

WHERE THERE IS sorrow there is holy ground. The preacher must tread sensitively. It is tempting to leave it to music, readings and prayers to match the varied moods of those who mourn. But our service today[1] would not be complete without an attempt to put into words of a direct and personal character the sympathies of a nation, and to articulate the faith for which this cathedral has stood over the centuries of our island story.

First we want to express our solidarity with the families and friends of those who died in this disaster. For them the tragedy remains, and with it the numbness of loss and grief. The tragedy was so sudden – the loss so unexpected. To those who carry this burden of pain we offer our deepest sympathy. And no sympathy will, I know, be so heartfelt as the sympathy of those who shared the horrors of that night but came through unhurt, and with their families and friends unharmed.

Not even the firmest faith is enough to insulate us from the pain of loss and grief, or from that sense that, with the death of someone dear to us, our own life has lost its meaning. *Time* must help. It is said that you must survive in grief through the course of a full year before life begins to knit together again, and threads of purpose begin to appear. Those of us who have friends who are in sorrow must give them time, and with it the chance to speak of their sadness. We must not only be ready to offer our words of comfort – we must also be ready to listen patiently to their words of grief. There are moments, of course, when we are so overwhelmed that we can say nothing. There is no reason to be alarmed at that. The better part of mourning, better even than patience, is *silence* – silence which touches the edges of the grief which others must endure. Patience and silence and time – and standing beside us through all is God.

To some who mourn, the question is bound to arise, inevitably,

---

[1] Sermon at the Memorial Service in Canterbury Cathedral on 15 April 1987 for those who died on the Zeebrugge Ferry.

bitterly perhaps: *Why* should this happen? *Why* should a good God let it happen? I do not believe that they will be easily satisfied by argument or explanation. In suffering and bereavement we know that no theoretical answer will do. Hearts cry out not for answers but for friends who will share suffering with us. The stilted, agonized-over lines in a letter; the tongue-tied neighbour who is content just to sit with us – these are the things which count.

In this disaster it has been the practical, down-to-earth support given by so many doctors and nurses, rescue-workers, company officials, police and clergy which has struck us all. Even in the darkest moments at Zeebrugge there were rays of light – light in the instinctive co-operation of helpers from our neighbour nations; light in the gallant rescue work of divers, helicopter crews, harbour workers; light in the extraordinary courage of sailors and passengers who risked and sometimes lost their own lives to save others. Some of this light has already become legend. I think of the seaman who found that his diving gear was obstructing his search. So he discarded it, and stayed down in the dark until he found three lorry drivers, trapped alive in an air pocket. I think of the passenger with spinal injuries carrying his baby daughter to safety in his teeth. I think of the four men trapped in lower decks taking turns to hold above water the head of an elderly woman. I think of the man who acted as a bridge to allow others to crawl across, and the grandmother who tried to save someone in a falling wheelchair.

These are but a few examples of human heroism which this disaster encouraged and inspired. There are many, many others, and some will never be known. Our whole nation joins today with those who were rescued at Zeebrugge in admiration and gratitude for all who saved life at sea, or brought kindness and comfort on land. We owe a special debt to our friends in Belgium – the total commitment and excellence of their rescue and hospital services figure in every account I have heard or read. As so often in the past, tragedy at sea has displayed the human qualities of courage and generosity in all their splendour.

In the last century a terrible earthquake struck Italy. An eyewitness described 'the wreckage and ruin, the apparently blind and stupid carnage inflicted by sheer physical forces'. In the midst of it moved a man carrying two small children: 'Wherever he went he seemed to bring order, hope and faith in that confusion and despair.' The eyewitness said that he made them feel 'that somehow love was at the heart of all things'.

Someone who was in the midst of things at Zeebrugge said later: 'Tragedy does not take away love: it increases it. Perhaps we are more loving people, more sensitive, more concerned for each other because of that moment of grief which overthrew our ideas of what things matter, and opened our eyes again to the importance of our common humanity.'

It is in the selfless heroism of so many at Zeebrugge that we can see God's love at work. For the God and Father of our Lord Jesus Christ is not a God who stands outside us, and sends disaster. He is not even a God who offers comfort from a distance. He is Immanuel, God with us, the God who in Christ crucified plunges into the darkness of human sorrow and suffering, to stand alongside us, even in death.

Christian faith does not mean believing in impossible things. It means trusting that Christ's promises never fail. 'Though a man die, yet shall he live.' Faith is not hoping the worst won't happen. It is knowing there is no tragedy which cannot be redeemed.

These things we shall remember again on Good Friday. On Saturday, on the night before Easter Day, we shall light the Easter fire in Canterbury. A large single candle is lit from it and carried into the Cathedral. With the shadows of the vast vaulted roof above us, it seems such a little, vulnerable thing – and yet it is there, making its way through the darkness, and, as other candles are lit from it, a pool of light and hope begins to spread. Such is our faith and hope in the risen Christ. Not a hope which ignores the shadows of suffering and death, but a hope strong and secure in the assurance that love is 'at the heart of all things', that the eternal God is our refuge, and underneath are the everlasting arms in which are held those who have died, as well as those who mourn their loss.

Those who died at Zeebrugge did not die deserted by God, abandoned by him in an alien element, far away from his care and love. Though for a few who died their graves should be the sea bed, nevertheless they are as truly in God's loving hands as if their bodies lay in the most gracious of country churchyards. There also his right hand shall hold them in death as in life. That is the faith of the Bible.

There is no more beautiful expression of this faith than some words of the poet who wrote the book in the Bible called 'The

Song of Songs'. I hope those of you who have suffered loss may be able to take these words home with you, and keep them close to your troubled minds and grieving hearts. The words are these: 'Many waters cannot quench love, neither can the depths drown it.'[2] Many waters have not quenched your love for those who died. How much less shall the waters quench God's love for them, the God who gave them power to live and be yours – and who gave you the power to love them.

In the words of St Paul to companions physically and emotionally distressed,

> In all these things we are more than conquerors through him who loved us. For I am sure that neither death, nor life, nor things present, nor things to come, nor height, nor depth, nor anything else in all creation, can separate us from the love of God in Christ Jesus our Lord.[3]

To that love we commend all those who died at Zeebrugge. To that love we pray for all those who mourn them. Amen.

---

[2] Song of Solomon 8.7.
[3] Romans 8.37ff.

Dresden

And the Lord shall judge among many people and rebuke strong nations afar off and they shall beat their swords into ploughshares and their spears into pruning hooks; nation shall not lift up a sword against nation, neither shall they learn war any more. But they shall sit every man under his vine and under his fig tree and none shall make them afraid: for the mouth of the Lord of Hosts hath spoken it.[1]

THE PROPHET MICAH'S vision of peace is the theme I have chosen for this address.[2] What could be a better theme for our meditation this Sunday when we remember the dead and maimed, not only in the two World Wars but in the terrible succession of smaller wars which continue to distract our world. And what better place to speak about this theme than in Dresden. This city has suffered so much in war, but now it has a reputation as a centre of peace-making. I bring you greetings from another centre of peace-making, from your twin city, Coventry, in England which was also tried in the fire of aerial bombardment. In Coventry Cathedral as well Christians of many Churches will today be keeping a Sunday of remembrance and pledging themselves to another year of work for international reconciliation. They will be praying, like us, and meditating on the vision of Micah.

It is not possible to be a follower of Jesus Christ if you do not long for peace. Our Lord said: 'Blessed are the peacemakers for they shall be called the Children of God.'

We long for profound peace. The absence of war guaranteed by the coercion of the great powers does not measure up to the vision of Micah. We long for a world where order is supported by justice between people and nations and where every man is content and able to work among his vines and to sit under his fig tree. We long for peace and justice to nourish one another in a

---

[1] Micah 4.3-4.
[2] Sermon at the Kreuzkirche, Dresden, on Remembrance Sunday, 13 November 1983.

way that produces the possibility of plenty for all men and women. We long for this benign spiral upwards, but we see so often the malign spiral downward – injustice feeding conflict which can devastate the earth and produce poverty and hunger.

Truly to long for this peace with our whole heart is to be cautious about easy speeches which come too cheaply. There is much Utopian talk about peace; peace, where there is no peace. This talk is shallow and promotes cynicism. Christians believe that the truth is that this world is in rebellion against God. There is a profound egoism in individuals and a demonic complexity in the relations between groups and states which make easy talk about peace impossible.

The source and centre of the world is God, but individuals and groups try to live the lie that it is really they who are at the centre and demand that the world and other people revolve around them. This egoism inevitably brings individuals and groups into conflict with one another. Our Lord says, 'Blessed are the peacemakers for they shall be called the Children of God'. It is also true, however, that only those who see and understand themselves to be God's children and have God as the centre of their world can be freed sufficiently from egoism to become true peacemakers and truly at peace. The slogan of the Christian workers for peace in this country, 'Gott über alles', is the root and heart of the matter. No peace, no sense of human brotherhood, will last without a profound experience of the Fatherhood of God. This does not mean, of course, that Christians are unwilling to co-operate with others who have a sincere desire for peace, but we should never conceal our conviction that the deepest and most lasting peace is something 'the world cannot give' – it flows from a right relationship with God. The Christian workers for peace in this country have been an inspiration to so many people in my own land and all over the world precisely because they have never surrendered to easy talk but march instead under the banner of 'Gott über alles'. The world stands in such great danger, however, that we must seek allies among men and women of good will everywhere.

This generation has been given two signs which have burned themselves into the human imagination all over the world. These signs are 'the planet' and 'the cloud'. By 'the planet' I mean this earth, sapphire blue and beautiful, photographed from the moon and seen whole as never before in history. By 'the cloud' I mean the mushroom cloud over Hiroshima.

The vision of the earth as a whole helps to deepen our awareness of the essential unity of our planet. We breathe the same air, and pollution of the atmosphere threatens us all. New global communication means that we can speak peace or hate to one another more powerfully than ever before. At an economic level, a world economy is developing towards ever greater interdependence. Our world is a spiritual and material unity. When we injure our neighbours, we injure ourselves in many different ways. The longing for peace and unity reflects the real terms on which we live together on this planet.

The cloud, however, reminds us of the volcanic forces which threaten to tear the world apart. Those forces lie in nature but also in the hearts of men and women. Even though the vision of the planet gives us hope, we cannot be complacent about the cloud. Since 1945 we human beings have lived with the possibility that our whole species could be obliterated. We have made a great advance in technology without a corresponding advance in moral sense or understanding.

The Christian Church cannot just lament the evils of the day; we must work urgently and strenuously for a new way. We must fight against complacency and any callous acceptance of the present reality as anything but madness. A number of so-called developed societies are spending their best brains and a very large proportion of their resources planning for lunacy and destruction. This is a world where children are dying of hunger while we continue to pour our best efforts into preparing for Armageddon.

The Church has a special responsibility to foster truth and love in the world and this means a religious war on hygienic words which feed complacency about the dangers that face us and a war against the propaganda and the distortion which increase hostility between nations. The language we use creates the context and determines the character of the decisions we take. There must be an end to the sterile abuse between East and West which poisons language and turns other human beings into sub-human monsters.

Our Lord Jesus Christ said, 'Love your enemies, do good to those who persecute you'. This saying is still difficult for many people to accept and it is what forfeited Jesus the support of the revolutionary party in first century Palestine. But 'Love your enemies' is a credible peace strategy and one that the Church is specially authorized to pursue. At the same time we should support any effort to bring greater stability to our world and to build more effective international institutions to reflect our perception of one world as we see it in the photograph of the sapphire blue planet. We should, I believe, be paying more attention to the plea contained in the first report presented by the Secretary General of the United Nations Señor Perez de Cuellar. He described what he called 'the new international anarchy' and listed some steps which governments ought urgently to consider: greater use of the United Nations mediation facilities; more immediate resort to the Security Council and the building up of the United Nations policing capability. The Secretary General is talking about the provision of arrangements for the world which are possessed by the humblest local authority and certainly by the City Fathers of Dresden – an ambulance, a fire brigade and a police force.

A new world order is not, of course, only a matter of a more efficient police force. We should not forget the contention of the International Commission assembled by Willy Brandt that the denial of justice to the poor and hungry in the world will have more and more explosive consequences from which none of us will be entirely insulated. This is another direction in which we should seek to develop the capacity to feel and act as citizens of one world. It is not that we have to abandon a patriotic love for our own homeland, but we should try to transcend national self-interest as the only determining factor in policy.

All this sounds as if it is a matter only for the people at the top and those in positions of power and influence. The search for peace, however, must embrace us all. When the Pope visited your twin city of Coventry, he preached a sermon reflecting on the cathedral which had risen out of the ashes of the Second World War, and he said: 'The Cathedral of Peace is built of many small stones. Each person has to become a stone in that beautiful edifice.' Our prayer as Christians must always be, 'Lord reform the world but begin with me'. Jesus showed us a way of bringing peace into the world which has a relevance for family life, life in the factory and in the street. He teaches us the way of absorbing violence. He shows us open hands, pierced with nails. The open hands of the Lord and of his Church are a contrast to a sign more favoured by the world – the sign which was the salute of the Roman Army of Jesus's time: the clenched fist. In our daily lives, as Christians, we are called upon to forgo the way of the clenched fist, and to be open-handed, both generous in our love and accepting of the violence of a world in rebellion against its maker. The clenched fist, of course, wins victories of a kind, but whatever is built in this way soon crumbles like the Roman Empire itself, whose ruins and fragments litter the shore of the Mediterranean. It is not enough to say that we share the vision of Micah and that we want peace if we are not in our own lives as Christians prepared to follow the open-handed way of Jesus Christ and to accept its cost in suffering.

There is a legend of a modern man who went up to the angel behind the counter in Heaven and said, 'I am tired of war, violence, greed, lust and cruelty – I want peace, love, trust and joy', and the angel behind the counter replied, 'We don't stock fruits, only seeds'. The Christian Church is a colony of the next world in the present and we, as Christians, have the responsibility to cultivate the seeds of that next and better world which will more faithfully embody the vision of Micah and the vision of the PRINCE OF PEACE. There are no short cuts if we really long for the profound peace of God.

And may that peace, which passes all understanding, that peace which the world cannot give, may it keep your hearts and minds in the knowledge and love of God and of his Son Jesus Christ our Lord.

End of the Second World War

MOST OF US over sixty can remember where we were, that late-summer Sunday in 1939, when we heard that the United Kingdom was at war with Germany. If we search our memories a little further we can remember something else: the mood of the time. There was a certain relief that the period of waiting was over. But there was very little jubilation. We already knew too much about war for that. Memories were too fresh. After the Somme and Passchendaele we were not victims of any great illusion. We knew that war was ugly, but it was the lesser of two evils.

One of the great nations of Europe was in the grip of a regime that set at nothing the liberty, the dignity, the life of all those who stood in the way of its notions of racial superiority and the expansion of its territory. Diplomacy had failed. By the summer of 1939 the choice was clear. Germany's European neighbours either had to submit to Nazism or resist it by force.

Today[1] we thank God that with the help of our allies that resistance culminated in a victory in which the Nazi regime perished. No historical enquiry has suggested that Nazism was less wicked than we thought it in 1939, or that any other method than war could have brought it down.

The cost was heavy in a war which engulfed Europe, and extended far beyond it. And there are those present here today to remind us of the horror and heroism of the war which stretched into the Far East. Many of us will have personal memories of friends and relatives who died or who were maimed. The outstanding courage of those who were disabled is a constant reminder of the cost of our victory.

It was a war which claimed victims among combatants and civilians alike – the very old and the very young. One of the most moving memorials of the war I have ever seen is in Leningrad where a million people died during the siege. In the little museum attached to the cemetery for the war dead there is a tragically

---

[1] Sermon in Westminster Abbey on 8 May 1985 to commemorate the fortieth Anniversary of the end of the Second World War in Europe.

matter-of-fact diary, spread out page by page, written by a very young girl describing her life during the siege. She saw most of her family die of starvation. She survived long enough herself to be evacuated from the city over the icy road only to succumb almost immediately to the effects of cold and malnutrition. There are stories like that in almost every country of Europe.

It is right that we should remember the pity of war. Today, in this place, it is fitting that we should remember the sorrows of the United Kingdom in particular – the lives lost or laid waste, the treasures obliterated. But it is also right to remember the good that can be set against the grief. Part of the Christian answer to the eternal riddle of evil is that great afflictions call forth great virtues, public and private. Today we remember those virtues gratefully and humbly before God. We remember the steadfastness and unity of the nations that came together in the allied cause. So many of them we rejoice to see represented here today. We remember the qualities of our own sailors and soldiers and airmen: the loyalty they showed to their units and to their friends; their endurance of hardship and danger. There is a proper pride which says: 'Those people belong to us, and we to them, and we are glad of it, because they show what humanity can achieve.'

I remember very vividly during the Liberation of Holland coming with a squadron of tanks to the banks of a river. The bridges had been blown up. On the other side there was a village, and suddenly I saw the parish priest marshalling his parishioners, and encouraging them to bring out their furniture and to throw whatever they had into the river to make a causeway for our tanks. They emptied their houses. I was moved and humbled. They had already suffered so much during the occupation, and yet they were ready to rise to a new sacrifice.

Sacrifices there were on *our* home front, and we also remember the spirit that pervaded that. It was a sense of common cause transcending differences of status or interest. We recognized how precious our freedoms were and learned how much they cost. It was a summons to everyone to put a brave face on private pain, so that the face of others should not be clouded.

We remember faces, perhaps, most readily: the faces of our national leaders, serene in Buckingham Palace, even after it had been bombed; indomitable in Downing Street; and we have our own private memories of those countless people who made a duty of cheerfulness.

Some people question now whether the war was really necessary, and whether anything was achieved by the victory. I respect their freedom to make such a judgement, but I profoundly disagree with them. It was not a panacea for every ill. But the victory which closed down Belsen, Buchenwald and Auschwitz is in itself sufficient cause for thanksgiving. The war has also given us a forty-year breathing space in Europe, and the time has not been wasted. The peace settlement after the First World War nourished deep resentments and a desire for revenge. We can all rejoice at the contrast which is provided by evidence of genuine reconciliation after the Second World War. Old enemies have become friends in active co-operation.

The city of Coventry is a place where the reality of this reconciliation can be powerfully experienced. The charred ruins of the old building, destroyed by bombing in 1940, stand side by side with the new Cathedral. What often moves visitors most is the cross in the ruins, and the simple words, 'Father forgive'. It is a message which frequently brings British and German ex-servicemen together in shared emotion.

Such experiences can dent the lazy cynicism about humankind and the capacities of the human spirit, which undermines our work for a wider peace. Of course, the victory of forty years ago did not destroy all the world's evils. Every generation has its own problems to solve, and fresh forms of evil to resist. There is no retirement from the service of God, or from the struggle to establish his reign of love and justice upon earth. The organized life of groups and nations continues to be a struggle to dominate or to avoid domination. The appalling dangers of this, at a time when our capacity for destruction is so immeasurably greater than it was in the Second World War, are obvious.

Much has already been achieved in the reconciliation of ancient enemies. May our celebration of this achievement provide the energy needed to work for the greater world-wide reconciliation on which lasting peace depends.

This magnificent service is a gift offered to God, a gift of thanksgiving, penitence and hope – especially, the spirit of hope. We offer it in the spirit of Jesus Christ: he is at the heart of it. He said: 'First be reconciled to your brother, and then come and offer your gift.'[2]

---

[2] Matthew 5.24.

The Corrymeela Community

SOME YEARS AGO I remember standing, far from here,[1] by the most recently built big bridge in the world. It was in Istanbul and it joined Europe to Asia, linking one diverse people and culture to another. It was built by a consortium of several nations and across its span passed people of every race and tongue. It seemed a great symbol of hope. Then I noticed that every fifty yards or so stood an armed guard: there had been so many threats to blow up the bridge from those who despised the idea of the human race growing into one family. This was indeed a powerful image of the modern world – a world divided between bridge-builders and bridge-breakers.

Nothing is more important than that the Church today should be numbered among the bridge-builders. This is at the heart of our faith. Jesus Christ built a bridge between God and man, giving a human face to man's ideas of the divine. Inspired by the Spirit, we are called to build bridges between Christians, for divisions between Christians have always cost lives and betrayed the gospel. We are, too, to be bridge-builders within the community in which we live, for Jesus Christ is not just Lord of the Church, but Lord of all.

I noticed something else about that bridge in Istanbul. On one side there were the shanty dwellings and bazaars of the old world, and on the other the high-rise flats and the Mercedes cars of the new. It was a bridge between the old world and the new. That reminded me that Christians who pray 'Thy Kingdom come' must always be building bridges out of our history and into our future. Bridge-building, between God and man, Christian and Christian, the Church and the world, the past and the future – this is the heart of Corrymeela.

I speak to you as one who has some Irish blood and mixed

---

[1] Sermon at an ecumenical service at the Cathedral of St Nicholas, Newcastle-upon-Tyne, on 10 March 1985, the Sunday set apart for prayers for the Corrymeela Community of Belfast.

marriages in my family, and I have learned to love that country and know the affection it arouses. Countries, like individuals, only prosper if they are loved. Jesus the Jew wept over his native Jerusalem. He knew and understood our loyalties. He wept in affection, but also in sorrow for the misuse of the past. 'To understand the man', say the Chinese, 'you must know his memories' – the same is true of a nation. The Troubles in Northern Ireland are a complex product of a complex past.

History and memory, which can produce a proper pride in knowing who we are and where we come from, can also spawn the twisted mythology which lends credence and conviction to the narrow bigotry and idolatry of faction and sect. Bad myths exaggerate the faults and atrocities of the other side, and place a halo of romance around the heroes and martyrs of one's own. *My* religion, *my* country, *my* slogans, *my* territory, *my* ends and means – right or wrong! This is the diseased, self-righteous loyalty which can issue in the terrorism and brutal disregard for human life we have seen yet again in recent days. Those who will not face the *truth* of history are forced to repeat its tragic errors.

Bad myths leave a legacy of half-truths and false stereotypes which fan the fires of prejudice and hatred. People are judged by their labels not themselves: 'The Army', 'The Police', 'Catholics', 'Unionists', 'Republicans', 'Brits', 'Prods' – such labelling creates the tunnel vision which divides and despises others as scapegoats to be shunned or destroyed. And so a vicious circle turns and turns again in a spiral of cruelty, violence and despair.

The crushing weight of history and myth can paralyse the present, until (in Shakespeare's words) we are 'cabin'd, cribb'd, confin'd, bound in to saucy doubts and fears'. The present Troubles in Northern Ireland have lasted over half a generation – more than twice the length of the Second World War, and fifteen times longer than the Civil War in the South which followed partition. There are grown-up, married people in Ulster who have no memory of a time before this war; there are youths now in prison who were not yet at school when the Army arrived. For them violence and death have become a way of life. A young Derry lad staying at Corrymeela was asked what he normally did on a Saturday afternoon: 'We go down to the bookies. There is nowhere else. Or maybe there'll be a riot. If it wasn't for the riots [he added] life would be dead boring.'

Such history leads to what is perhaps the gravest of all

obstacles to those who would build a bridge to a new future: the apathy, cynicism and intransigence which come when people and communities with the richest of human qualities are so trapped by the burden of the past that the will and determination to change are smothered, and somehow even suffering becomes tolerable. When energy to build a better future is absorbed like this, society stagnates and decays. Riots and maiming continue with all the cruel logic of revenge, and give rise in turn to marital breakdown, illness, alcoholism, unemployment and poverty.

Yet it is precisely this deadlock, this paralysis, which Christ came to shatter, in order to set us free. In the miracle of Christ's birth, his life, death and resurrection, God has broken into history and snapped the chain of crime and recrimination. In Christ there is a new creation, a new beginning for humankind, with new power and new dimensions. In Christ, a bridge has been built between man's broken history and God's new future of faith, love and hope.

In his life and ministry, in his teaching and healing, Jesus shows us the life of the Kingdom, a life full of surprises, full of unexpected possibilities. Jesus' life is a life of love – love shown in bringing comfort to the bereaved, hope to the desperate, courage to the fearful, healing to the wounded, and wholeness to the broken in mind or spirit. Jesus was at home with all manner of men and women. He never allowed himself to be confused by the label or side-tracked by this or that party line or public image. The friend of Roman, Greek and Jew; the teacher who thought up a provocative story about a *good* Samaritan; the weekend guest of Pharisees who yet seemed to behave like a pagan on the Sabbath day; the intimate friend of women who were by no means all they should have been. Among his inner band of disciples were a publican and a zealot. He was indifferent to custom, and hostile towards it when it formed barriers between men or became an excuse for inhumanity.

A life so disturbing was bound to meet opposition, and even death. But that death only proved his life's unquenchable power – here was no end, but the beginning. Through the miracle of his resurrection and through the gift of his Spirit, new life, new vision, new purpose, new love, new energy were released into the world and the new community of the Church was born.

In and through his Church the love and healing, the peace and forgiveness of Christ, should be found today – for the Lord is here; his Spirit is with us. The Church should be the signal to the world of God's new age, his new creation in Christ; a bridge to new hope and vitality:

> What life have you if you have not
> life together?
> There is no life that is not in
> community,
> And no community not lived in praise
> of God.
> . . .
> You have seen the house built, you
> have seen it adorned . . .
> It is now a visible church, one more
> light set on a hill
> In a world confused and dark and
> disturbed by portents of fear.[2]

And this is *Corrymeela* – a light set on 'The Hill of Harmony', in a land confused, dark and disturbed by fear. First and foremost Corrymeela is a Christian community, a place of daily worship and prayer. Christ is the source of its light, power and unity. Each year the community kneels in dedication and affirms together: 'We surrender ourselves to the spirit of Jesus to overcome our divisions and make us instruments of his peace.' Corrymeela is built on the rock of conviction that 'it is Christ who has made us one, and broken down the dividing wall of hostility'. To this truth Corrymeela bears daily witness.

To the peace and beauty of Corrymeela come men and women from all walks of life – young and old, Catholic and Protestant, from North and South. They come united at first by at least a common experience of suffering, confusion and fear, and by a desire to find some meaning, purpose and hope. But Corrymeela is not just a haven for victims of violence – it offers something far more positive, practical and permanent. At Corrymeela there is support for families, old people and handicapped. There is work with groups of different denominations, children among them. And there is constant dialogue between people of varying beliefs who would not, and often could not, have met otherwise. People learn to live together, to listen and understand, to forgive and accept one another, to pray together, to shatter old prejudices,

---

[2] Eliot, T.S. 'Choruses from the Rock', *Collected Poems 1909–1935*, pp. 164, 179.

and to glimpse in Christ the vision of a new and better future. 'The more we talk together, the more we realize that our problems are caused by ignorance', said one group of Catholics and Protestants. 'Here in Corrymeela we listen to each other and learn from each other. We have also learned to disagree and yet remain friends.' Building bridges of healing across chasms of bitterness and division – this is Corrymeela.

What is this against the sheer enormity and resilience of Ireland's troubles? What can this tiny country community achieve where so many other solutions seem to have foundered? It is easy to be defeatist and cynical, but cynicism here is misplaced. For the power of Corrymeela is the power of Christ, a power made perfect in weakness. It is most often in the small and ordinary things of life that God begins to show himself most clearly: the stable at Bethlehem, the tree on Calvary, the empty tomb in Jerusalem. It is often through homely incidents and meetings in our own lives that we first sense the presence of God calling us to follow him. 'He who would do good to another', wrote William Blake, 'must do it in minute particulars.'

Repeatedly Jesus spoke of the Kingdom of God as a seed. He spoke about a sower whose efforts at scattering seed met with various setbacks, and about how some of the seed produced a rich harvest. He spoke also about how seeds that are sown grow unnoticed, through the quiet action of God, even while we sleep. And he spoke of the Kingdom as 'like a grain of mustard seed which a man took and sowed in his field; it is the smallest of all seeds, but when it has grown it is the greatest of all shrubs'.[3]

So, small beginnings like Corrymeela are not to discourage us – on the contrary, they speak eloquently of the way of God and his Kingdom. An old Russian saint declared that the man with peace in his heart could convert the countryside for 200 miles around. Already, after just twenty years, there are signs that Corrymeela is growing fast. Many have been touched and healed by its ministry. Many more have been inspired and encouraged by its story, and have joined the swelling ranks of supporters, of which the Corrymeela Link is an effective reminder. Today, in many churches, Corrymeela Sunday is being observed with admiration and enthusiasm.

It has been said that Corrymeela is an attitude of mind, not just

---

[3] Matthew 13.31–2.

a place: it can never be contained by walls or limited to localities. It is an attitude founded in faith and grounded in prayer; an attitude with divine power to build impossible bridges – and transform the world.

The South Atlantic Campaign

Jesus said, 'Let not your hearts be troubled ye believe in God, believe also in me'.[1]

THE EVENTS OF the summer of 1982 have left us all with strong and vivid impressions.[2] We have heard and read and seen moving stories of courage and restraint, comradeship and unsentimental realism. We are in no doubt about the professionalism and humanity displayed by our forces. They deserve our gratitude and admiration.

For those directly involved in the South Atlantic, and for those who through it suffered pain and loss, memories today will be many, fresh and sharp. I still think of the young wife of a marine, interviewed on television with her children as her husband's ship sailed from Portsmouth. 'How do you feel to see him go?', she was asked, 'It is his duty to fight', she said, 'He is doing his job – he will be all right.' He was among the first to be killed. It is primarily to those people and for those people I try to speak this morning.

Memories need managing – even memories of the happiest experiences and the people we love most. For with memory can come the awareness of that experience or that person as no longer present. And in that awareness can lie sadness, nostalgia, a sense of loss. As for memories of bitter experience and people who have wronged us, if unmanaged they too can be a source of continuing pain and guilt.

To manage memory is not to turn our back on it and resolve to forget. That drives memory underground to become a source of unease. Often, too, there would be a lack of faith, a failure of love and respect, in resolving to forget. The past has too great a power and too strong a claim on us to let us simply renounce it and put it behind us. Equally, of course, to manage memory is not to live in the past – clinging so tenaciously to yesterday that we can see no

---

[1] John 14.1.
[2] Sermon in St Paul's Cathedral on 14 June 1985, at the dedication of the Memorial to those who served in the South Atlantic Campaign.

good in the present and no hope in the future. No: managing our memories means realizing that what is past is neither *fixed* for ever nor *lost* for ever.

Our response to the past is not necessarily fixed, finalized, unchangeable. Something may have happened which is painful and bitter, and for a while the memory is equally painful. But as time passes there may begin to grow out of what has happened, out of that bitter root, something that is not bitter at all. We begin to see a loved one's life in a new light. We recall the best memories. We view the achievements and the promise afresh. We remember the love and affection, given and received. So, slowly, a new mood of gratitude and acceptance defeats the memories of bitterness. It is important to be aware of this at a time when memory is still painful.

And to manage our memories is also to understand something even more important: that the past is not *lost*. What is past from our point of view has not faded into nothing, or fallen for ever into a bottomless pit. For there is a point of view, a perspective, other than ours – the perspective of eternity, the perspective of God.

To see with the eyes of eternity is to see all the past and all the future together in one timeless, everlasting present. God *cannot* forget. God always looks *at* those people on whom we can only look *back*. God *sees*, now and always, those faces we can only *remember*. So, our memory of a beloved face is not a lingering after-effect of what used to be. It is a glimpse of what God sees now. Our memories are not fading photographs of what was once in the world – they are moments of insight into what is present to God now.

It is fitting that on the memorial which we are about to dedicate there is inscribed the name of each one of those who died in the South Atlantic. This signals a deep truth of our Christian faith. Jesus Christ never spoke of the masses, mankind, the multitude. He spoke of a certain man, a certain woman. And in mingling with every sort of person he made them feel that they mattered – because they mattered to God.

The memorial is not simply an expression of the nation's respect and gratitude to those who gave their lives. Still less is it a substitute for the personal and affectionate remembering of those who loved them in the past and love them still. The inscribing of each name makes a great statement – a statement of faith, the statement that each honoured name recorded there still has someone who owns it. Each inscribed name is the name of someone who *is*, someone who lives in the sight of God. God sees each one of them still. And God sees *with them* us who remember. And God sees what he can bring about, for us and for our world, from what they achieved in life and death, and from what they suffered, and from what we, who mourn them, have suffered.

So this loving remembrance, here where their names will stand, is far more than a backward look in time. It is an enduring reminder of the love and mercy of the Almighty and Eternal God: Father, Son and Holy Spirit.

'Jesus said, "Let not your hearts be troubled; believe in God, believe also in me".'

The Oxford Movement

Whoever eats this bread shall live forever.[1]

THAT GREAT DISCIPLE of the Oxford Movement, William Gladstone, recalled travelling as a young man on the outside of a stage coach where he overheard a snatch of conversation between two of his fellow travellers: 'Well,' said one, 'what *is* the Church of England?' 'The Church of England', said the other, 'is a damn big building with an organ inside.' When Keble and his friends had done their work, such a utilitarian definition was not possible. The Church is a divine society in which heaven and earth and all the centuries meet. She is nourished and sustained by the eucharistic food we receive today and given her character by feeding on the body and blood of our Lord Jesus Christ. Today,[2] we celebrate our communion with those fathers of the Oxford Movement, particularly John Keble, who opened the eyes of so many to the mystery of the Church and who protested at her degradation.

Keble himself lived with a profound awareness of God's presence in the Church, and by his preaching, poetry and person reminded some of the best of his contemporaries that it was not sufficient to think of her as a merely useful institution; a department of state; an educational or welfare agency, or a society for the improvement of morals.

Appealing beyond his own time and place to the evidence of the springtime periods of Christianity, in particular to the scriptures, seen through the eyes of the fathers of the primitive Church and the Anglican divines of the seventeenth century, Keble – probably unwittingly – stimulated a movement back to the Christian roots that released great energies in the Church of England. Men and women were given strength and grace to spend their lives in gruelling missionary work in the great new

---

[1] John 6.58.
[2] Sermon delivered in Oxford on 16 July 1983 on the occasion of the 150th Anniversary of the Oxford Movement.

cities of industrial Britain. Vast numbers of churches, schools, nunneries and almshouses remain as a testament to the vigour which flowed from the Oxford Movement. Christian poetry and art, beauty in stone and glass, brought into the world of getting and spending a sense of the delight that there is in the presence of God.

Keble, his friends and followers, kept open the channels of communication and inspiration which flow from God and from the Church of all the centuries at a vital moment. He preached his crucial Assize sermon on 'National Apostasy' in 1833,[3] at a time when a new, post-Christian view of the truth and meaning of things which had no place for the presence and activity of God was growing in potency and confidence. This view derived its authority from the scientific world picture of the Enlightenment and it was pitted against the traditional, Christian understanding of the meaning of the world and the place of human beings within it in a stark and vivid way. In the Assize sermon, Keble imagines the spokesman for this alternative view as saying of Christian doctrine: 'Once and for all we will get rid of these disagreeable, unfashionable scruples which throw us behind other people in the race for worldly honour and profit.'

Over the past 150 years, the clash has perhaps become moderated and less explicit. Religion has been pushed even further out of the centre of the picture into a sphere of private life where it affords psychological satisfaction for some who are built that way. For much of the time, the Church has consented to this exile to the comfortable periphery; that, in fact, is where we find ourselves now. One of the most common defensive comments you ever hear as a clergyman is, 'I think religion is very much a personal matter'. This is no doubt true on one level, but often what is being stated is a denial that God has any claim on us or any right to be taken seriously as an element in our understanding of history or social affairs.

The Church has lived so long and so comfortably in its privileged privacy that sometimes it comes as a shock to realize that we live in a country, most of whose citizens subscribe to another religion. It is often not perceived to be such and, like many very powerful systems of thought before it, the truths of this modern religion are commonly believed to be self evident.

[3] 14 July 1833.

One of the central beliefs of this West European creed, which is given almost unquestioning assent, is the notion that 'the individual has a right to happiness'. Our contemporary secular religion also nourishes the hope and expectation that this happiness can be a possibility for the whole world.

I do not wish to sneer at this modern religion. In many ways, the modern creed is humane and admirable with a vast amount of achievement to its credit. Nobody wants to return to a world in which the conditions of life for the mass of the population were nasty, brutish and short. Anyone who presumes, however, to speak from a Christian pulpit must say that biblical Christianity does start from a radically different point of view and has different emphases. I passionately believe that Christianity is a better description of reality than its secular alternatives and does in fact nourish human beings in all their God-given dignity. I also believe that this contrast is becoming more and more evident.

Very briefly, I wish to place side by side some of the central ideas of the modern creed and biblical and apostolic Christianity.

The modern creed starts with an 'individual' who possesses all that is needed for making moral choices and for personal development. Biblical Christianity, on the other hand, begins with man's dependence on God. Men and women do not grow to their full stature until they surrender their own 'rights' in the service of the love of God and the neighbour. The service of God, as the Prayer Book reminds us in one of its noblest prayers, is perfect freedom.

In the modern creed, happiness can be achieved by consuming and possessing, although there is now increasing cynicism about the claim that man can live by bread and circuses alone. In the Bible, however, joy and fullness of life is the gift of God which comes to some of those, like the poor in spirit mentioned in St Matthew's Gospel, whom modern man would count most miserable.

One of the ways in which the modern creed is being revealed as increasingly threadbare and exhausted is the ebbing of the element of hope in it. The modern creed used to be full of hope that it was possible to attain on earth by rational organization and the advance of technology a Utopia of independent individuals in a world-wide society of plenty. This hope, in gradual progress and the beneficence of technology, has evaporated, leaving large numbers of people immobilized by fear and anxiety.

The biblical vision of deepening conflict, leading to darkness in which God will inaugurate a new era – the pattern seen in the life, death and resurrection of Jesus Christ – appears once more to be in tune with the times. As Keble said, in his great sermon 150 years ago: 'The churchman is a man possessed of an unfailing, certain hope; he is calmly ... sure that the victory will be complete, universal, eternal.'

There is a missionary challenge in this contrast between the modern creed and biblical and apostolic Christianity which could be indefinitely extended. This challenge is addressed, not merely to members of the Church of England but to the catholic and universal Church as a whole. Our membership of the Church gives us access to a divine reality through the bread of eternal life, which is not made stale by any passing fashion or contemporary orthodoxy. In the Church of England, at a time when we were in danger of being assimilated to passing fashion and conditions, Keble and his friends recalled us to the inheritance of all the ages which we share and taste in common with others who are members of the one, holy, catholic Church.

Keble was the most reserved of men. He would not have wished the 150th anniversary of his sermon and his serious appeal to an apostate nation to have been marked by an after-dinner style of reminiscence or something merely historical. He bent all his powers to reflecting the divine life which he received as a member of the Church and through the bread and wine. He protested against the subordination of the Church to a system of belief reared on different foundations from those we find in the Bible and the apostles. He rejected the idea that the Church should merely be a useful agency in the service of the State.

We are not faced with precisely the same problems. There is very little danger now that the State would even wish to see the Church as a yoke-fellow in its activities. We are, however, faced with the danger of the Church becoming just a Friendly Society in a culture whose public structure of truth and meaning excludes God and centres on the autonomous individual. There is, for us, a danger that Christian doctrine could become so attenuated that the divine reality will be diluted into a dull echo of the liberal consensus.

In its own day, the Oxford Movement stimulated a great missionary effort to our own country and culture. We need to do this now – it is the best way of celebrating 150 years of Tractarian influence. This is by far the most important field of missionary endeavour in our own day, because, being missionaries at home, we are engaging with that West European secular dream which has penetrated to every part of the globe and overturned almost every other culture in the world.

This missionary effort is not something for the intellectually gifted alone. Keble perhaps taught more effectively in the sweetness and gentleness of his life than in his preaching. We are in Oxford. We need thinkers in every department of life, ready to challenge our present decaying assumptions. But we follow Keble most surely by being missionaries of love, showing in our lives what it means to put the centre of self outside self, and what spiritual beauty follows. The world is once again waking up and needs to hear this truth.

So be of good courage. We are meant to praise a movement that goes on, not to bury it. Be hopeful. Be loyal to your Church. Be thankful to those who have gone before you in the faith, but above all be thankful to God who gives us the body and blood of his own Son to nourish us in the way and give us a foretaste of heaven.

The Seventh Earl of Shaftesbury, 1801–85

> Inasmuch as ye have done it to one of the least of these my brethren, ye have done it unto me.[1]

THE FUNERAL OF the seventh Earl of Shaftesbury[2] in October 1885 provided one of the strangest scenes of the Victorian era. Nothing like it had been seen since the nation had said farewell to the great Duke of Wellington, thirty-three years before. Then royalty and statesmen had come to honour a great military hero and the streets were lined with substantial citizens. But in 1885 it was almost wholly poor people who came. There were costermongers and bootblacks, flowergirls and matchsellers, climbing boys and crippled children – a whole gallery of Dickensian characters stood in the pouring rain to salute his passing. All wore black, if only a scrap of rag. Children from societies with which he was associated followed the procession carrying banners proclaiming: 'Naked, and ye clothed me', 'A stranger, and ye took me in.' The presence of these children 'was especially appropriate at the obsequies of one who had ever been the friend and benefactor of the young'.[3]

Here was no political demonstration or orchestrated lobbying. It was a spontaneous and heart-felt reaction of the kind now reserved for royalty. *So why?* What sort of man was it who attracted such a warm response? We must beware of pat answers – Lord Shaftesbury was the kind of public figure whom it is tempting to pigeon-hole. He easily attracts labels, 'the greatest English social reformer' or 'the worst kind of puritan paternalist'; 'a manic depressive' or 'an evangelical saint'. Yet he defies such classification, and we belittle his stature by trying to sanctify or sanitize him.

His was certainly no simple or uncomplicated character. Consider some of the contradictions. Heir to an earldom who,

---

[1] Matthew 25.40.
[2] Sermon at a service of thanksgiving in Westminster Abbey on the occasion of the centenary of his death, 1 October 1985.
[3] *The Times*, 9 October 1885, p. 12.

after Harrow and Oxford, completed the Grand Tour and entered parliament as member for a pocket borough. Many recognized in him a future Prime Minister. In parliament he staunchly opposed the Reform bills of both 1832 and 1867. Yet Lord Melbourne described him to Queen Victoria as 'the most dangerous Jacobin in Your Majesty's dominions.' He stands in history as the poor man's earl – the people's champion, but he had to bolt and bar his door against those same people after he had stopped military bands playing in parks on Sundays. His diaries show frequent depression at the thought that he was not appreciated, had no friends, and lacked sympathizers.

Deeply ambitious though he was, he consciously and courageously abandoned hopes of a political career to sponsor a bill to regulate working hours for children in factories. He worked tirelessly for that cause and yet incurred the wrath of his supporters when he accepted a compromise. He gave his energies both to public campaigns we would applaud, and to acrid ecclesiastical disputes we would sooner forget.

Shaftesbury was an uncomfortable figure. He possessed an intensity of feeling and commitment we would find difficult to take. I suspect we should compare him more with the prophet Jeremiah than with some popular social reformer. In despair at the opposition he encountered in speaking up for his Lord, Jeremiah declared:

> So the word of the Lord has brought me insult and reproach. But if I say 'I will not mention him or speak in his name', his word is still in my heart like a burning fire, shut up in my bones. I am weary of holding it in; indeed I cannot.[4]

I think that passage captures the character of Shaftesbury. And I believe that from him we can learn the *cost* of doing justly, loving mercy, and walking humbly with our God.

The rightness of Shaftesbury's causes seems transparent to us now. It was not so then. The opposition was often plausible and powerful. Shaftesbury had to refute that opposition, whether from respected experts or self-interested bigots. His own father condemned him for fomenting revolution. He faced the constant and exhausting grind of drafting, lobbying and speaking; of taking a step forward only to see it soon reversed. Like some stubborn prize-fighter he would raise an issue in parliament, be

[4] Jeremiah 20.8–9.

defeated, and return doggedly to the fray. It was, for example, in the early 1840s that he took up the cause of chimney sweeps' boys: it wasn't until 1875 that he finally saw success. The Ten Hour bill to limit the working day was not passed until fourteen years after he had introduced it.

Some things never change. However good the cause, there is always hard slog, disappointment and frustration ahead – the appeal that flops; the meeting that nobody attends; the speech that is misunderstood. Those of you here today who are involved in promoting reform and changing public perception will know what it means to feel committed to an idea whose time has clearly not yet come. Shaftesbury drew on deep reserves of faith and the certainty that he was doing God's will. He made his own the famous prayer of Saint Ignatius Loyola:

> Teach us, O Lord, to serve Thee as Thou deservest; to give and not to count the cost; to fight and not to heed the wounds; to toil and not to seek for rest; to labour and not to ask for any reward save that of knowing that we do Thy will.

The enduring causes and achievements we celebrate today need no elaboration. Their story is well known – they speak for themselves. So let me point to four *principles* that seem to distinguish that achievement: they are principles from which we still have much to learn.

First, Shaftesbury was not afraid to select unfashionable causes. Think of the one to which he gave perhaps most time throughout his life – that of humane provision for the poor insane. There was not much kudos to be gained from bearing the title 'Metropolitan Commissioner in Lunacy' – yet it was a post he filled for 57 years until his death. He saw the need, he took up the cause, and he stayed loyal to it. 'There is nothing poetical in this duty,' he commented, 'but every sigh prevented and every pang subdued is a song of harmony to the heart.'

Second, a simple point – Shaftesbury got his facts right. This was not always straightforward. He undertook the dangerous journey down a mine-shaft in an open bucket to see conditions for himself. He knew accidents were frequent, but commented in his diary: 'Thought it a duty: easier to talk after you have seen. So away I went and had ever in my mind, "Underneath are the everlasting arms" – so I feared not.' A more succinct combination of fact and faith would be hard to find. Anyone pronouncing on issues must be ready to answer the question 'What do you know about it?', and answer with information, familiarity and conviction. Lord Shaftesbury and his friends got at the facts. He is described as showing 'microscopic philanthropy' which catches it well. For him Christians charity demanded a compassionate inquisitiveness. Ignorance was no excuse.

Third, Shaftesbury always made it clear on what basis he was acting. He was a man driven by a special kind of Christian vision which, kindled in childhood and quickened by experience, went far beyond the conventional pieties of his day. We may not find all his theology sympathetic, but there is no doubt he lived it to the full. If asked 'Why should a Christian be involved in this or that cause?' his answer would have been clear and definite. Every person should be able to live life as a child of God, with proper freedom, justice and dignity. Where there is poverty, oppression or ignorance, we who are better off should accept some responsibility and duty to take action. What is morally right cannot be politically wrong and what is morally wrong cannot be politically right. These are good principles, but the crucial point is that for all his practical involvements, he never lost sight of them. Christians involved in social concern need this sort of framework and need to keep returning to it.

Finally, Shaftesbury was not afraid to show passion. He had boundless sympathy and concern for the down-trodden and deprived, and when pleading their cause he didn't mince his words. 'I cannot feel by halves' he said. He and his like saw how grim city life had become and wrestled with passion to bring this home to people who never saw it, didn't live anywhere near it, and couldn't imagine it.

It is easy enough to admire these principles. But Shaftesbury's achievement was to *act* on them, with courage and conviction, and show what can be accomplished in the name of the Lord and for the sake of his kingdom.

Today, a century after Shaftesbury's death, there are few of us with such moral or spiritual stature. Yet the need in our society for more 'humanity mongering' (that is his phrase, not mine) has never been greater. There is much unfinished business. The horrors of child abuse are not, alas, confined to mid-Victorian England. There are still many who suffer daily what Shaftesbury called 'the scorn and neglect manifested towards the poor and helpless'. Although conditions of work have improved dramatically, opportunities for work continue to recede and we are being constantly warned of how our cities, like Shaftesbury's London, are all too often combustible places of despair, disadvantage and decay which can explode in riot, brutality and crime. Above all, we need individuals as well as institutions to exalt altruism against egoism, community against self-seeking, charity against want. We need to be reminded that there is a transforming power at work in human affairs which can change intractable situations and bring new life into the darkest places.

It is the lesson of a once well-known prayer that all our deeds and all our speeches without charity are worth nothing, but that given this divine sustaining energy, immense creative and renewing forces are available to the Christian community which in the past have moved history and will move it again. Our secular generation may have forgotten most Christian truths, but perhaps it has remembered just sufficient to judge our words by our deeds and to measure them both by the example of him who bestrides history, who took the form of a servant and said: 'Inasmuch as ye have done it to one of the least of these my brethren, ye have done it unto me.'

Lord Shaftesbury achieved precisely that, and Gladstone's words inscribed at the foot of Eros are both a tribute to his life and work and a stirring challenge to us all:

> During a public life of half a century, he devoted the influence of his station, the strong sympathies of his heart, and the great power of his mind to honouring God by serving his fellow men . . .

The Ordination of Women

WE ARE ALL influenced by our own circumstances in the debate[1] about the ordination of women. How you perceive it depends very much on where you started. I entered the debate in 1975 as a bishop, responsible for our international conversations with the Orthodox Church. I felt it necessary to issue warnings of the ecumenical consequences of taking steps which might gravely hamper these conversations. It seemed to me that although there were some theological reasons in favour of the ordination of women, it was not right in principle to take such a step at variance with the unbroken tradition of those who hold to the threefold apostolic ministry without much further consultation and deeper theological considerations.

Since the debate in 1975 a good deal of this has taken place. Some have proceeded to ordain women. None of them have – as Churches – regretted the step and I have some experience of these Churches.

The Lambeth Conference of 1978 was not, as some predicted, the break-up of the Anglican Communion. It could be argued that we emerged with a great self-understanding of our identity as Anglicans and with a clearer experience of the sources of our dispersed authority. Also, perhaps, a better understanding of its strengths and weaknesses. There is certainly more enthusiasm and preparation for the Lambeth Conference of 1988 than for its predecessor.

In 1978 and 1984 there were further major debates in Synod against the background of continuing and stronger ecumenical conversations which had not foundered as a result of developments on this issue. Indeed they have taken the questions on board. We have also just now taken steps to admit women to holy orders in the diaconate.

In 1984 I still felt it right to vote against our proceeding to

---

[1] Speech in the General Synod on 26 February 1987, on the Report of the Bishops on the Ordination of Women to the Priesthood.

legislate, the Synod decided otherwise; and that is why we are here today. I hope I can be acquitted of dogmatic haste or inconsistency in my approach to this question. I am therefore sorry the House of Bishops' Report before the Synod today has been the occasion of what I can only call premature panic.

I want to remind General Synod of just what the House of Bishops' Report actually entails – and what it does not. In November 1984 the General Synod resolved to ask the Standing Committee to bring forward legislation to permit the ordination of women to the priesthood in the Church of England. The McClean Report *The Scope of the Legislation* set out various options as to how this could be done. Some of them seemed to some of us to be more about the dismemberment of the Church of England than the ordination of women. Last July in the debate on the McClean Report the bishops decided – with the consent of the Synod – to do some thinking of their own about the legislation the Synod had called for. The Synod now has before it the *unanimous* Report of the House of Bishops.

I stress its unanimity. The House believes that if the Synod wishes to ordain women to the priesthood, *this* is the way it has to be done. Some bishops are strongly in favour. Others are equally against. Others still are agnostic on this issue or inopportunist. But we are unanimous that if the decision of the Synod of November 1984 is to be carried into effect, it must be along some such lines as these. In the unlikely event of the Synod unanimously accepting the House of Bishops' Report, we would still not have taken the decision to ordain women to the priesthood. I want to underline this both to the Synod and to those listening to it and reporting on it. The actual decision to ordain women to the priesthood will only have been taken when a draft measure and canon is given final approval.

A draft measure and canon could at the earliest come before Synod for general approval in February next year. Then it would go to the dioceses before returning to the General Synod. Final approval would, of course, necessitate two-thirds majorities in each House. The most optimistic estimate for this debate would be July 1991. This is the earliest that the Church of England could actually make its decision. But there may well be delays. There would almost certainly be a call for a separate debate in the Convocations and the House of Laity. With time allowed for passage through Parliament and the Royal Assent the earliest possible date for actual ordinations would be July 1992. It could take two years longer. It is therefore a little early to be taking the tarpaulins off the lifeboats – or even signalling to other shipping to stand by to take on board some of the passengers.

So *this* debate is still about what should or should not be in the legislation the Synod has *already* asked for. It is not yet that women shall or shall not be actually ordained to the priesthood. Furthermore the opponents of the ordination of women will, I hope, gain some comfort from the careful listing of the theological issues which still remain unresolved.

It has frequently been alleged that the Synod's resolution in 1975 that there are no fundamental objections to the ordination of women obscured the fact that there continue to be theological issues for debate. The bishops intend to continue work on these issues. We do not promise immediate or easy solutions. But we take with utmost seriousness the particular role of the bishops as teachers and guardians of the faith and instruments of the Church's unity.

A working party consisting of bishops, both those for and those against, has already begun to discuss the theological questions. Much attention was given to these theological questions by the whole House when it debated the Report. Great care was taken to state them in such a way that people with deeply held convictions could recognize them, but also that they should be seen to be balanced and fair by those of opposite convictions.

Whatever individual members may think of the particular strengths or weaknesses of the theological arguments deployed in my exchange of correspondence with Cardinal Willebrands, it is clear that we have to take seriously the official reserve of the Roman Catholic Church – as well as listening to the theology of other ecumenical partners. The bishops gave a prominent place to this kind of discussion in our Report. ARCIC will also be taking it on board as it proceeds to look at the reconciliation of ministries.

The Report is quite clear that there is no way forward to be found in parallel episcopates or competing jurisdictions. I, for one, do not intend to preside over the abolition of diocesan episcopacy and the parochial system as the Church of England has known it from the time of my predecessor Archbishop Theodore of Tarsus. Ecumenically, it would be more disastrous to jeopardize the episcopal nature of the Church of England than to move towards the ordination of women to the priesthood. I do not want the Church of England to slide into a kind of episcopal congregationalism. This would certainly be to betray our catholic and Anglican heritage. I believe that those who once favoured the exploration of a 'Continuing Church' are now less enthusiastic. A parallel body claiming to represent the true Church of England is really a non-starter. The 'Continuing Churches' in South Africa and the USA are not happy examples.

But what of those – a substantial minority – who continue to have grave reservations. The bishops have never said – certainly not in this Report – that those with serious objections to the ordination of women must get out. No one is being asked to leave. But the bishops do recognize that some may feel in conscience obliged to sever communion with the Church of England – even though the majority deny that this is justified. Those who leave may claim that they represent the traditional faith and believe themselves to be entitled to some of the resources of the Church of England. While the bishops note that some may so claim and so believe, they do not themselves endorse this. It is one thing to recognize such an attitude, it is another to say that such people are right. The financial provisions the bishops speak of is not therefore compensation. Nor would it apply to parishes or congregations.

The bishops see the importance of safeguards for those who cannot in conscience acquiesce in this development. There are clear safeguards for parishes and priests, and for dioceses and bishops. As far as I can see, there are none for archbishops – perhaps we don't have consciences!

Because the norm envisaged by the bishops would be that the Church of England ordains women priests – if it does so decide – it has been said there will be no room for bishops who prefer not to ordain women to the order of priesthood. This is not true. It is said that a bishop who did not ordain women would be an anomaly. But, as the section on safeguards for future episcopal appointments makes plain, a diocese could ask for a bishop who would not ordain women to the priesthood and the House of Bishops recommends that a bishop ought to respect the mind of his diocese on this matter as expressed in its diocesan synod. This would be an interim anomaly lasting as long as there is deep division on this subject within the Church. What would not be acceptable is for such a bishop to go further and deny that the Church of England as such ordains women to the priesthood. If I, as a bishop, am in communion with another bishop, then I must recognize as priests all those he ordains and all those our Church ordains – even if I remain uneasy about this development and refrain from doing so myself. The Bishops' Report does not recommend a monochrome Church of England. It legislates for untidiness, but the Church of England is no stranger to that.

Now, as to the manner of our voting on the Resolutions. It is clear that those who favour the ordination of women to the priesthood will vote in favour of them – even if they have some anxieties about safeguards. For example, what will happen to women who believe they have a vocation to the priesthood in a diocese which does not ordain women. Then there will be some, perhaps a larger number than either the protagonists or the protestors realize, who still remain agnostic – either by reason of the balance of the theological arguments, or perhaps because they are waiting for a wider ecumenical consensus before seeking a change in practice.

Similarly there will be those who believe the arguments in favour now tip the balance, and who do not believe it is impossible for a woman to be a priest, but who remain doubtful as to timing for ecumenical reasons or because of a concern for the unity of the Church of England. I confess to being such myself. If I were being invited to vote on the legislation today, I would still want more evidence of consensus in the Church of England. But whatever its weaknesses I believe in a conciliar method of Church government; I believe in debate and discussion. That will continue if we see the Bishops' Report as the right basis for the Church of England's eventual decision about the ordination of women. I believe we should now move to test the mind of the Church. This can only be done against actual legislation. This is why I shall be voting in favour of the motions today.

We owe it to the women who ask for their vocation to be tested. We owe it to the rest of the Anglican Communion – I see the Bishops' Report as a document that will go to the 1988 Lambeth Conference as the Communion continues to debate the matter. We also owe it to the Roman Catholic and Orthodox Churches to take our decision on grounds of catholic order. If this decision is to be made, it must not be made on the basis of a change in the character of priesthood but as an expansion of eligibility to the priesthood. If we pass the motions today it will be for the bishops and Synod to see that this is made plain.

What then of those bishops, clergy and laity who are convinced that it would not be right in principle for the Church of England to ordain women to the priesthood in the foreseeable future? No doubt they will be bearing in mind the fact that if the motion is voted against today, it cannot be moved again in the remaining life of this Synod. I have to say that the issue is unlikely to go away, but I recognize that there are those who sincerely believe that such a delay would ultimately be for the good of the Church. I do not believe the evidence from the dioceses justifies that. If I am wrong, this will clearly be shown when a draft measure and canon goes to the dioceses.

As we come to this debate today we need to recognize the very strong feelings on either side. We need to be careful to respect the integrity of each side. There will be no absolute victors. There will be those who will be hurt and wounded.

The Bishops' Report hints of the long and often controversial stages by which a doctrine or practice is eventually received by the whole Church. Some of us remember the debates about the Church of South India. I remember it being said there would be an exodus of over a thousand clergy if we entered into communion with that Church. Even ARCIC - sometimes accused of erring towards the bland and ideal - speaks of 'conflict and debate'. Catholic-minded Anglicans can gain some consolation from the fact that the dissension between conservatives and radicals on the nature of bishops at the Council of Trent became so heated that the rival delegations not only branded their opponents as 'damned heretics' but fell upon each other afterwards in the streets to the extent that blood was shed.

It was John Henry Newman who said: 'You cannot have Christianity and not have differences.' In spite of and in the midst of our deep differences on this question we can still claim to be the Body of Christ. The Church remains the Temple of the Spirit. In this recognition we come to listen to each other, to the voice of Scripture and tradition, reason and experience, and to cast our vote.

Many of those on the edge of the institutional Church - and some of those within it - are bewildered by the very strong passions this debate has generated. In parishes lay people seem to have other priorities – communicating the faith in a largely secularized society, ministry to people in desperate need, or giving Christian education to our children, maintaining the inspiration of Christian worship. I have received two letters of complaint to the effect that 'the vicar preaches of nothing else now but the ordination of women'. One comes from a parish where he is against it and the other from a parish where he is for it.

Perhaps this fact gives us something in common, whichever way we vote today. For in the last analysis Church order is at the service of the mission of the Church. Those in favour will see the ordination of women as developing and completing the wholeness of the threefold ministry for mission in today's world. Those against it see it as an invasion of contemporary secularized culture, thus obscuring mission. A common recognition of the primacy of that mission will hold us together even in our differing judgements. Neither campaigning nor threatening in the end of the day will serve the unity or mission of the Church unless we are more deeply committed to God and to each other in bringing the gifts of Christ to this generation. In the end of the day our strength is not in the wisdom of men (or women) but in the power of God. If we seem to be at a loss for a solution to our problem at the moment we should do well to remember that the strength of God can be made perfect only in recognizing our weakness.

Morality in Education

I WARMLY WELCOME this opportunity to talk to you[1] on this important topic. I do so, not only as a Christian, but also as a school governor, a retired teacher and fellow parent.

Let me begin with the obvious; in *our* 1984, not George Orwell's literary fantasy, something far more serious threatens us than the attentions of a Big Brother. It is a profound crisis of confidence in *all* our institutions – political, economic, social, religious and educational – as sources of public and private morality.

By morality I mean, of course, far more than mere morals. I mean a way of deciding and thinking how we should act, 'what manner of life we should live', as Socrates put it. Even for Christians this is no longer as straightforward as it seems. For many of us, and especially parents and children, it seems difficult – despite much loose talk about a revival of so-called 'Victorian' values – to find the right moral vocabulary at the right time. It is not merely that it is always difficult to affirm moral absolutes in a morally relative world. It is also that the *lingua franca* of morality – Truth, Justice, Goodness, Fairness, Conscience and so on – has become weakened and debased by the shrill psychobabble of 'consensus', 'experts tell us', 'research shows', etc. This really *is* Orwell's Newspeak – as dubious as it is dangerous.

Behind this, of course, lie more profound changes within our society itself. It seems to me that – like Archimedes and his bath – we are trying to displace one set of moral values by another set which are intrinsically far less 'moral'. For example, fundamental questions about sexual morality are now treated – in the school, the media and often in the home itself – with a kind of moral neutrality, as if they were a branch of civics or home economics. Similarly, in politics, we seem to be returning to a world where political morality is based on pragmatism, not principle, and

---

[1] Address to the meeting of the National Confederation of Parent-Teacher Associations held at the University of Kent at Canterbury on 14 April 1984.

whose moral vocabulary is often the bomb rather than the ballot box, the death squad rather than democracy. Even in our domestic politics, I sometimes feel that the moral force behind what T.S. Eliot called 'well-being in community' is being gradually weakened by belief in a crude individualism, excessive collectivism, or purely economic objectives.

Finally, although you do not need an Archbishop to tell you this, Christianity in general and its Churches in particular, has lost much ground – to psychiatrists, social workers and telly pundits, for example, and to the state – as the arbiter of private and public morality. And, although I regard this situation as by no means irreversible, and while I do *not* believe that today's morality is wholly detached from Christianity (much of the language of secular ethics – doing good, gaining self respect, etc. – is still deeply rooted in Christian symbols and images), it is also clear to me that Christianity has now largely ceased to exercise *supremacy* over what little is left of the moral domain. In short, I think we are confronted by what is at worst a moral vacuum and at best a morally shapeless world for ourselves and our children to inhabit. Which way, then, must we turn?

One answer, of course, is to turn towards those time-honoured sources of moral authority, the family and the school – so strongly represented here today. But I am not at all sure if the traditional equation of age plus experience plus knowledge equals authority really convinces us any more, let alone our children. For, by itself, adulthood no longer confers automatic moral authority.

This is not simply because more and more of our children (and a good many adults too) seem to have become the prisoners of a culture devoted to what is new and what is young. Sometimes this is all to the good, if only because old ideas and stereotypes need to be challenged to justify themselves. But it can also lead to a mindless commitment to novelty for its own sake, a devotion to the ephemeral and the superficial. Such children may well reject old and apparently arbitrary values, irrespective of their objective merit. Many too, and with more justification, will point to the sorry state of the adult world and say to us, 'This is where your so-called values have got us. The sea and the land are poisoned; children starve while others live in luxury; and over it all hangs the cloud of Hiroshima. This is the world you have made with your values; what's so great about that then?'

Such questions put us on the spot morally. We may reply that it is precisely because our values have been neglected that the world is the way it is. But as adults we cannot really escape that way, because our children say, 'But the men who are doing these things go to church on Sunday and pray to the same God as you, and then on Monday morning carry on as usual'. The charge against the adult world is thus hypocrisy, as well as incompetence.

Another aspect of this is very personal to the lives of individual teenagers. I know that the clergy have recently been advised to give up politics for Lent, but I am afraid that the problem of teenage unemployment must be regarded as moral as well as political and I make no apology for including it among the factors which have led to a diminution of respect for traditional authority. Parents and teachers may exhort their children and pupils to work hard for exams; encourage them to prepare themselves to play a responsible role in society. Yet how can it not sound so very hollow when we know, and they know, that half of them may find it impossible to get the jobs which give reason to all that homework and which make sense of adult notions of social responsibility? Unemployment does not, of course, provide a reason for neglecting homework: quite the opposite; nor does it provide any excuse for children to run riot, sniff glue or turn to theft. But it is one more factor to undermine adult guidance, adult authority, the adult world which presumes to command yet cannot deliver.

If all adult authority is now in question, parental authority is especially challenged. It is very difficult, nowadays, to cast the family in its traditional role as the creator of moral values. Of course, I do not think there ever was a golden age of parenthood where parents wisely enunciated and children uncritically accepted parental fiats on moral issues. Nor am I denying that, in some ways, the change has been beneficial. The parent has gone from being the stern arbiter of a child's life to being a friend and companion, to whom the agonies of adolescence can be communicated in the knowledge that the parent will understand, sympathize and even talk frankly about their own problems at that time in their lives. In my youth, it never occurred to me that my parents had been through problems similar to my own and I would, I confess, rarely have confided in them.

But there is another, less cosy, side to this. It is that the progressive erosion of parent power, especially in the last thirty years, has left a moral vacuum in many young lives. It is not so much that parents have lost their ability to offer moral guidance to their children; it is that they have lost their nerve. Many feel that their responsibilities have been assumed by others – directly by teachers, social workers, youth leaders and other professionals, and indirectly by television and popular culture. I know that there are plenty of adolescents who, when they have a problem, prefer to pick up a telephone and dial Capital Radio's *Help-Line* rather than talk to their own parents. Children, I suspect, sense this moral vacuum, even if they do not always admit to it.

Yet it is also clear to me that our education system is equally ill-equipped to uphold and communicate morality. Indeed, it is difficult to inculcate morality *through* education when one finds so little morality expressed *in* education. Its traditional, Platonic rationale (to shape values and morals) has, I think, been corroded by two powerful contemporary trends. One is the tendency to judge the value of education solely in terms of the demands of the labour market. As a friend of my daughter told me, sadly, on her last day at school, 'I came here hoping to be educated, and all I seem to have been doing is a five-year aptitude test!' In any case, there *is* no labour market for many young people, especially the so-called under-achievers of our inner cities. Indeed, the real moral challenge may be how to educate such children creatively for non-employment rather than how to feed them an increasingly irrelevant dose of the Protestant work ethic.

In such circumstances, reinforced by overcrowded classrooms, chronic indiscipline and diminishing resources, it is unsurprising that even committed teachers – and there are plenty of these – tend to retreat either into barren professionalism ('salaries and dinner duties', as a teacher put it to me recently) or cynicism and despair. The net result – and this is the second corrosive trend that I see – is not only a diminishing sense of vocation but also a diminishing sense of responsibility for teaching moral values at all.

So many moral issues, whether public or private, are either sacrificed on the altar of moral indifference (i.e. sitting firmly on the fence) or evaded altogether ('I don't think we have time to discuss that now, have we?'). If teachers – and parents – are unable to respond swiftly and honestly to moral issues, then how on earth can we expect our children to? The brutal paradox is this. Just at a time when, as I suggested earlier, a clear morality needs to be communicated to our children, the two best agencies available for this, the home and the school, are often unable, and in many cases unwilling, to do so.

How then can we, as parents and teachers, seek to reassert primary moral concepts in such an amoral world? Clearly there is little sense in blindly attempting to reimpose yesterday's morality. But we can surely strengthen the formal context within which moral education – in its widest sense – takes place. We can, for example, seek to strengthen the family, not only as an institution but as a source of guidance and values. Perhaps we have been over timid in reasserting parent power. I am not suggesting, of course, that we, as parents, become more punitive, merely that we accept our responsibilities as moral educators and take them very seriously indeed.

Within our education system, we must build up the pressure for a more explicit moral dimension to the curriculum. Since the days of Plowden and Newsom, there have been, as you will know, a number of consultative documents and experimental projects aiming at precisely this. Some have been relatively influential. But I personally feel rather uneasy about much of what passes for moral education. Much of it is almost wholly secular in conception and content – the prisoner of current intellectual fashion. There is no ethical or credal core to it. I think also that it is a mistake to give moral education too specific a slot in the school timetable, a set period every week, to be dreaded in advance by pupil and teacher alike. We need to point more to the moral dimensions of *all* subjects – history, English, even physics – so that children learn to perceive moral situations not as separate from the rest of daily life but as an integral part of the human experience at all times.

But to 'pep up' the family and the school as sources of moral guidance will not in itself strengthen morality. We need clear structures as well as good intentions. Indeed, as the Taylor Report (to which your association gave such valuable evidence) made clear, truly effective moral education will only develop when there is a genuine working partnership between parents, teachers, children, local authorities and the state. All too often there is, instead, utter confusion as to who does what.

Perhaps some of you recall the headmistress, quoted in *The Times* about a month ago, who said:

> I hope the school's standards of morality are pretty clear to children but, if these are contrary to what they are learning at home, I do not think it is any part of the school's role to make it more difficult for a child to live with her parents. Ultimately, the morals of the home are what is going to influence them.

Sometimes, too, there is hypocrisy as well as confusion. The partnership is often no more than a token one, with the real power and decision-making lying firmly with the school and City Hall. Indeed, it is ironical that, just when parents are being encouraged to exercise more freedom of choice as educational consumers, they are also often reduced to mere token status in the educational decision-making itself.

This, you will tell me, is where the PTAs come in. And so you do, as a vital link in the partnership chain and in the process of moral education itself. Maybe you could do even better. Head teachers have often told me that the kinds of parent they most want to talk to – the unemployed father, the depressed mother, the indifferent, the hostile and the cynical – are the ones least likely to be found at PTA meetings. It often takes a real crisis – a threatened school closure, or a hard drugs outbreak – to pull such parents in. So clearly you must reach outwards into the community as well as upwards into the staffroom and the bureaucracy.

But there must always be more to morality in education than improved curriculum design and parent–teacher partnership. All of us who are trying to give children guidance for life will sooner or later be faced by the need for a belief or faith to act as a criterion. If morality is – to return to Socrates again – 'what manner of life we should live', then it needs *values* and it needs *vision*. It is precisely these which the Christian faith supplies. I do not just mean through formal, religious education in our schools, vital as this is. Nor do I mean the public statements on moral issues such as abortion, sexual deviance or nuclear weapons by people like me. I do not even mean evoking the phrase 'Christian conscience' – that crucial line between religion and morality – when the situation demands it. I am talking instead about the way in which the Christian faith supplies the answers to basic *educational* questions concerning the purpose of schooling and the values that education should reflect and convey.

The Church of England's National Society put out a recent and quite outstanding Green Paper entitled 'A Future in Partnership' in which it said:

Christ's pattern of disclosure also sets standards. It points up those human motives and drives that under the Grace of God will lead to what is good, what can in the end be perfect. Morals and values will not be created in a school by accident, nor should their fount be peremptory edicts from on high (the head teacher's notice at assembly, for example). They must be reflected in the life of the school in the simplest of activities – how people speak to each other, degrees of courtesy and helpfulness, how property is handled and resources shared, how to avoid the abuse of power . . . in selfish or restrictive ways . . . how talent and success is accredited without further belittling those who feel they have failed . . . Christian reflection will assist in the establishment of sound moral criteria . . . these will be caught long before they may be taught.

Beyond the school gates, too, the Christian faith can give purpose, and direction, and focus to every moment of one's life. It does not automatically resolve moral dilemmas, or make any less complex everyday matters of moral concern. But it does provide a language in which to discuss them, a leading light by which to see them. Indeed, there is a mounting body of evidence to show that many Britons, especially the young, now perceive and experience the Christian faith primarily in terms of its moral imperatives and as a guide to personal conduct. For Christianity can truly deliver us from ideas which are simply inherited from our teachers or which merely reflect our own prejudices. In Iris Murdoch's brilliant phrase: 'A man's morality is not only his choice but his vision.'[2]

The Christian vision of man, of society, and of the means of realizing both, should be as integral to moral education as Christian values. For example, the concept of partnership in education is more than just a PTA 'buzz-word' or bureaucratic device. It is also an essential part of the Christian vision of creation itself, which sees human beings very much as co-workers, or partners with God in the work of creation. As John Macquarrie, the Oxford theologian, so excitingly puts it, we are called to be 'stewards and guardians, co-workers with God and his other creatures in a creative venture that reaches beyond what we can imagine'. That seems to me not a bad description of what the education process ought to be about, 'a creative venture that reaches beyond what we can imagine'.

Similarly, the Christian faith can offer a perspective within

---

[2] Murdoch, I. *The Sovereignty of Good*. Routledge & Kegan Paul, 1970.

which revealed truth can become acquired truth and that acquired truth tested in the relationships of everyday life. It offers, in short, a vision of moral change. It is a vision best summed up in the Durham Report's clear call to the Christian teacher (and one which should be relayed to parent and teacher alike): 'If the teacher', it urges, 'is to press for any conversion, it is conversion from shallow and unreflective attitudes to life. If he is to press for commitment, it is commitment to . . . that search for meaning, purpose and value which is open to all men.' This seems to me to be one point from which it is possible to begin to talk about morality in more specific terms. That is – and this is some way from our traditional, Old Testament understanding of morality – by beginning with what one ought to do, rather than with what one ought not to do.

Since, in the popular mind, 'morality' always seems to mean 'sexual morality', I shall start with the problem of sexuality and young people. In fact, I have already begun, by referring to sexuality as a problem. It is not a problem in itself: it is a natural and essential part of human nature which is with us from the moment of birth to the moment of death. It is simply no good to pretend that it should suddenly arrive on one's wedding day. Yet even now those who try to understand and sympathize with young people's sexuality, and who try to explain that a mere reiteration of Christian morality is inadequate, are immediately accused of condoning immorality. It has to be faced that conventional moral codes in sexual matters are so widely, constantly and publicly flouted that a simple appeal to a return to Christian standards is, frankly, useless.

This does *not* mean, however, that we abandon the field to the advocates of teenage promiscuity, any more than the widespread use of drugs means that we should legalize their use. We must *not* abandon our principles. We must *not* surrender to what is less than the best. But it *does* mean that we have to find other ways of persuading our adolescents that early promiscuity, like drugs and alcohol, is morally, physically, mentally and emotionally damaging; that it distorts and spoils other forms of relationship; that it can degrade and destroy lives which have hardly begun: and that it is wrong, because of all these excellent reasons, and not because of any kill-joy instinct on the part of grown-ups.

We have to gain the confidence and respect of our children: challenging them to define and defend the meaning and purpose and values they want in their lives. They need the challenge of the adult as well as the love of the adult. And then getting them to discuss the implications of these values for the way they conduct their daily lives: relating them to what they learn at school, to what they read in the newspapers, and what they see on television.

Starting from this basis, parents can begin to stress certain absolute standards. Through explanation and discussion, parents can establish that children must not lie, or cheat, or steal, or hurt those weaker than themselves. They can emphasize the need to respect others, to help the old and the sick. Schools can give life to dull moral precepts by arranging for children to see the needs of others – by organizing voluntary work or raising money for local charities. And they can demonstrate the need for such precepts by showing children the plight of victims of crime and thoughtlessness.

Children also have to be made aware that life is always going to impose limitations and restrictions on them, that life is often unfair, that human advance does not come from slick patterns of management, or cosy notions of caring and sharing, but from facing up to problems and tackling them to the best of one's ability as and when they occur. This is the challenge of adulthood: but you must not forget the love – not the love that makes for softness, but the love which gives meaning and purpose to life and patience for the struggle and stress of it.

I would extend this point to suggest that a major purpose of our education system must be to build up the values and virtues which are vital to a home, or a school, or any community – a mixture of four in particular – and I emphasize that, as the advertisement goes, the beauty is in the blend.

First, there are the family virtues: acceptance, tolerance, compassion and forgiveness. They enable people to grow, and without them no community can thrive. Second, there is the discipline of mind and spirit – the proper use of talents. The family virtues on their own can be flabby and soft, keeping people in immaturity and dependence. Third, there is loyalty: loyalty can sometimes be narrow or complacent and then it deserves to be mocked. But, at its best, loyalty provides a nursery for our affections and no community can thrive unless it is loved.

The final ingredient is also a corrective of the previous one. I fumble for a word, but I cannot do better than 'vision'. There is a need for people, especially children, to know where they are going, to commit themselves to the venture, and to have the inspiration to make the journey. 'Without vision, the people perish.' Now these four ingredients: let us call them love, discipline, loyalty and vision. They are not exclusively Christian words – that is what I hope makes my talk open to those of other faiths too. But I do believe that religion can bind the blend together, and provide the spirit which enables it to mark a good family or a good school.

Love on its own can be too soft or sentimental. Discipline and standards can be too stiff and hard. Loyalty on its own can be complacent and narrow. Vision on its own can be theoretical dreaming. But fused together, they can make a family, a school, and a nation.

I receive many letters asking me to make moral pronouncements on certain subjects: to say, definitively, what is right and what is wrong. The problem is that the most serious and important things rarely allow such black and white thinking. To oversimplify can be as morally irresponsible as to deny any kind of moral dimension at all.

So we also need to teach our children to be sensitive to complexity, to be wary of making moral judgements until they know the full facts, and understand the full consequences of the decision they reach. It can sometimes be more important to *give* something to a situation than to make a judgement about it, and perhaps part of the genius of Christian faith is that it teaches us a reluctance to judge (for which of us should throw the first stone?) but to discover where to look for answers to complex problems: *how to transform a situation so that an answer can be found.*

At this point, I return to my quotation from the Durham Report: 'The search for meaning and purpose and value.' A moral education must meet all these demands. It must draw moral meaning from what it teaches; it must give children a sense of what is valuable both to them and to their family and community; and it must give them a sense of active purpose so that they can hope to transform the situations that life will throw at them. Too often we seem prepared to let children go out into a complex and often hostile world without a moral tool to make sense of it, and with which to tighten up the nuts and bolts shaken loose in even the calmest life.

Morality in education is not an optional extra, like art or music lessons. Nor is it something which can be left entirely to parents. Every family, every school, every community produces situations which require moral thought; parents and teachers, working together should make sure that our children are able to recognize these opportunities.

Fighting Divorce with Faith

CHURCH AND STATE seem to be whittling away at the stability of marriage. Lawyers may plead that they are operating more humane procedures. Churchmen may say they have to cope with the casualties. However genuine these claims, they do not convince the critics. This may be an appropriate time to restate some principles.[1]

The Christian Church did not invent marriage, which has its roots in the origins of mankind. It is a great human blessing. Christians have always known this but they have been subject to failures of nerve about it. They have worried that the physical union of a man and a woman cannot truly be the kind of thing of which their spiritual God would approve. So they tended to put all the emphasis on the obedient procreation of children, as if marriage were good only for populating the world.

Lately Christians have seen more clearly and said more distinctly that our physical natures and our emotional natures are worthwhile in their own right. There is and is meant to be much more to marriage than offspring. But it still looks as if we cannot entirely shake off the idea that God grudges us our joys and exacts a penalty for them. It is the permanence of marriage now, rather than its fertility, that we seem somehow to have turned into a price we have to pay rather than a particular blessing.

Christians know that marriage is 'for better for worse,' but sometimes this is made to sound more like a threat than a promise. It ought to mean 'whatever happens, we can count upon each other.' It is a travesty to make it mean 'even if we regret it we are still lumbered with each other for life.'

Can we wonder that the modern world is so divorce-minded when Christians give the impression that the point of marriage is to stay together whether you want to or not? When church people are asked what they believe about marriage, they are apt

---

[1] Article in *The Times* 2 July 1984.

to talk about the wrongness or the impossibility of divorce and its unhappy prevalence today.

But when the Lord was asked about divorce as a problem in his time, we are told that on the contrary he forthwith began to talk about marriage. The Pharisees, to test him, asked, 'Is it lawful for a man to divorce his wife?' Jesus replied that divorce is permitted in the law because of 'hardness of heart' but that marriage goes back to the creation. God's purpose is that man and wife shall 'become one'. So we see the Lord firmly putting divorce in its place.

We are right to be deeply concerned when marriages fail: concerned for the bitter disappointment and waste, and for the shock waves that spread into other people's lives. Sometimes there is someone to blame, but blaming is not much help. Putting asunder is not a sin like greed that people commit because they like it. To punish divorced people is no way to assuage their, or our, guilt. But mercy is not a cheap and easy alternative. Human mercy is always liable to a kind of soft corruption, unlike the mercy of God. One way we can recognize that God was in Christ is in the toughness of his forgiveness, the inexorable claim in his mercy.

Failure in marriage has always been a problem. Some of the reasons why it is an enlarged problem today are not bad reasons but good. People live longer; and they expect more of the relationship of marriage. We only need to look at tombstones in an old churchyard to see that until lately it was likely to be premature death that broke up homes. Two hundred years ago the average marriage could be expected to last fifteen years. Now the expectancy would be fifty years.

It is a lot to ask that two young people marrying in their twenties should vow to be faithful to each other for their whole lives, when they may easily live into their eighties; and when they have learnt to mean by 'faithful' not just docile and well-behaved, but romantic and companionable. Furthermore, women are seeking an identity which is not solely dependent on the family.

But many people are making these vows and meaning them and keeping them. As Christians we need not be surprised that life asks a lot of people. We have no right to go back on the demanding and inspiring idea of fidelity. We need to show it in action.

What we are asking for is not conformity but response. The great ideals, of which faithfulness is one, are great realities, not vague hopes. There would be no point in the Christian Church or anyone else 'upholding marriage' unless human beings were the kind of creature to whom lasting 'pairbonds' are fundamentally natural. When we try to enforce ideals, however noble, all we get is unfairness. They need to grow as a harvest with patient cultivation.

Preparation for marriage is not teaching engaged couples an eleventh commandment, 'Thou shalt not divorce'. It ought to be confirming and developing their own understanding and entering into their celebration. We offer them the possibility of a union of two lives in which dependence and independence enhance each other, in which love comes to mean more than romance but certainly not less, and much more than mere unselfishness.

No doubt there will continue to be disagreements and arguments about what to do when fidelity fails. But if we can communicate a positive understanding of marriage as it can be, as two people making a present of their whole lives to each other, so as to give each other unlimited scope to grow in mutual encouragement, that is what goes in the front of the picture and everything else can fall into place.

Society and our children desperately need good marriages. The law deals with fairness and with people's rights. The Church has to communicate a message about what Austin Farrer called 'the union of duty with delight'. We cannot expect the lawyers to do our job for us.

The Royal Wedding

HERE AT LAMBETH I can see through the trees of my garden, across the river to the spires and towers of Westminster. Today, 400 million people the world over will watch the Royal Wedding[1] on television or listen to it on the radio as it takes place there in the Cathedral. It is an inescapably public occasion. But, to a lesser extent, all weddings are very much public occasions.

A man and woman make their vows to one another in the presence of God and in the face of the congregation. We gather together to share their joy and celebration. There is no better wedding present for any couple than the assurance that, as they pledge themselves to each other before the altar of God, they are surrounded and supported by the sincere affection and genuine prayer of family and friends. That is a present for a lifetime. We are also at a wedding to witness and encourage because it is of vital concern to the wider community that marriages should be well-knit, and have the best possible foundations in the teachings of Christ.

Every wedding is a society wedding. I do not mean for the finery and glamour; but it is on the well-being of the family that society depends. It is the family, not the district or the nation, that is the real unit in human affairs. A man fights ultimately in defence of his own backyard – a woman saves to keep her children from starving.

It matters to all of us how life is transmitted to the next generation. The quality of the union which a man and a woman make when they commit themselves to one another in marriage will leave its mark on the future. If the partners seek to build up a life together which is full of love and trust and forgiveness, strong enough to withstand and to learn from the changes and chances of life, then friends will be able to refresh themselves in

---

[1] *Thought for the Day* on BBC Radio 4, on the morning of the wedding in Westminster Abbey of HRH Prince Andrew and Miss Sarah Ferguson, 23 July 1986.

the radiance of such a partnership. Above all, children will be nourished by example and atmosphere even before they are able to speak. They will learn to be trusting and loving in their turn.

The consequences of unstable, unhallowed relationships in which the partners are not working at building one another up in marriage, but are treating one another as objects or playthings, are only too obvious. Such dishonest unions leave a deep wound on the future, and disfigure the life from God that flows through us to the generations to come.

Many people nowadays are tempted to despair that life is too vast and complex and impersonal for individuals to make much of a mark. But in marriage a couple can exert the most profound material and spiritual influence on the future.

I know Prince Andrew and Sarah understand the seriousness as well as the joy of matrimony. They appreciate too, and every feature of today's wedding service will remind them, how gladly and generously God's gracious help is given to those who seek it at such a time.

Of course, we shall all enjoy the fun of the wedding – and quite right too. This is a day to celebrate the magic and the mystery of love. But each of us can also make a vow today to do everything we can to nourish and build up the stable marriages on which the future of our country depends. None of us today need feel we are mere spectators.

Huguenot Heritage

'IF GOD IS for us, who then can be against us?'[1] From these words the followers of John Calvin in the Europe of the 16th and 17th centuries drew courage and inspiration. In France, in face of bitter persecution, the Huguenots found strength to remain steadfast in their faith in God's power and God's love. 'Who shall separate us from the love of Christ? Shall tribulation, distress or persecution, or famine, or nakedness, or peril, or sword?' This was no empty rhetoric. What enabled the Huguenots to survive was a determination to trust in the sovereignty of God and his providential care, and a conviction that nothing can separate us from the love of God in Christ Jesus our Lord.

In our twentieth century desire to find paths of reconciliation between separated Churches, we can forget the bitter facts of mutual hostility and violent persecution which mark the conflicts of history. In the sixteenth and seventeenth centuries our forefathers in the faith made their opponents suffer in ways which appal and horrify us. Dean Church, Dean of this Cathedral, 100 years ago said: 'The deep hatreds and deep injuries of that time gave to the theological controversy an unfairness and a virulence from which it has never recovered, and which have been a disgrace to Christendom and fatal, not merely to unity, but to truth.' If in our own day the theological controversy has at last begun to recover, to change from polemic to dialogue, we must still remember that our ancestors could use the cruel weapons of intolerance. Indeed is it not a task for the scholars of our time to seek to understand how it could be that good and learned men were led to conclusions so much at variance with the Gospel of Christ. Would not that be a healing way of recalling the trials of those whose memory we revere today?[2]

[1] Romans 8.31.
[2] Address in St Paul's Cathedral on 26 September 1985 in Commemoration of the Revocation (16 October 1685) of the Edict of Nantes (13 April 1598), which had given Huguenots religious liberty.

To honour such courageous men and women is not, of course, to dispraise the many Catholic martyrs who saw truth from a different perspective and were in their turn prepared to die for their beliefs. We should be beyond partisan martyrologies, honouring the Huguenots as we honour those Roman Catholics whom a recent report reveals have been executed in Albania for daring to baptize children in the world's first officially proclaimed atheist state.

We think especially today of the first wave of Huguenot immigrants who came to Britain in the latter part of the 16th century. We think above all of those who arrived here at the end of the subsequent century, fleeing the events which stemmed from the Revocation of the Edict of Nantes, when all Protestant services were forbidden, all Protestant chapels destroyed, and all Protestant ministers banished.

The contributions those refugees made to enrich the life of this nation were many and varied. Tradition has linked them especially with the trade of silk-weaving. Certainly, they brought with them skills without rival in the England of their time. The Court of the Weavers' Company here in London recorded in 1684 of a piece of work produced for their consideration: 'This Court considered thereof, and conceiving the like hath never been made in England and that it will be of great benefit to this nation, do agree that the said John Languier be admitted a foreign master gratis . . .'

It was not only in silks that the French were experts. The manufacture of textiles was one of their specialities – the name of Courtauld stands today as evidence of their immense and enduring contribution. It is said that the Cardinals in Rome had to order their red hats from Huguenot felt-makers in Wandsworth. More substantially, many of the refugees were skilled craftsmen – to this the majesty and beauty of St Paul's bears eloquent witness. Others exhibited experience and acumen in commerce, education and the professions. In the City of London the Huguenots, exercising an influence out of proportion to their numbers, were intimately connected with the foundation of the Bank of England. The presence at this service of the Band of the Grenadier Guards reminds us of the Huguenots' loyal and distinguished contribution to the Armed Services of the Crown.

In many ways the Huguenots have added to the vitality and prosperity of England. They set fresh standards of excellence and put England in touch with new and progressive movements of thought and action. It would, however, be complacent to suppose that such contributions were made without dissent. Love for the stranger and appreciation of his special significance have been opposed in every age by the voices which cry, 'These strangers are a threat to our way of life. If we do not deal with them, they will take over'.

Toleration had to battle with popular suspicions that the French were stealing jobs from Englishmen. In a debate in 1693 on a bill for the General Naturalization of Foreign Protestants, Sir John Knight, MP for Bristol, asserted that England was being afflicted by the kind of plagues which fell upon Egypt – the kingdom, he said, was 'bringing forth Frogs in abundance'. He demanded that the bill should be kicked 'out of the House, and then foreigners out of the kingdom'. It is to the credit of parliament that his speech was sent to the common hangman to be burnt and strenuous efforts were made to organize financial relief for the refugees. As Bishop Compton of London declared: 'All men are not required to be wise enough to judge of the secular consequences in this accident in the peopling of our country – increasing manufactures, industry, trading and the like: but God excuses no man from being good and charitable.'

In and through their varied activities the religious energies and convictions of the Huguenots remained clear and paramount. Wherever they went they founded French-speaking congregations, organized whenever possible on the Genevan model. At the beginning of the 18th century there were no less than twenty-three French churches in London. Their relations with the authorities of the Church of England were generally amicable, though it was hardly possible that Christians who organized themselves on strictly Presbyterian lines should not at times have frictions with a Church governed by bishops. But the frictions were minor – the friendships were lasting. In the library of this cathedral there are the returns for public collections held in Cambridgeshire to support the refugees. In the whole of that county, only one parish failed to make a positive response.

It is a particular pleasure to me that one of the last Huguenot churches, with a record of unbroken worship from the 17th century, is to be found in the crypt of Canterbury Cathedral. There, in the Black Prince's Chantry, some thirty families continue to worship Sunday by Sunday, a reminder of the great contribution made by the Huguenots not only to Canterbury but to England as a whole.

The Huguenots were the first of successive waves of people fleeing from religious, political and economic oppression who have sought here a better and freer life. They have enriched this country which at its best has afforded them asylum and a tolerant reception in advance of the prevailing standards of their day.

It is easy to talk glibly about tolerance, particularly since so many of our present tolerant attitudes owe much to religious indifference and moral insensitivity. Cultures do not survive slothful tolerance of this kind for long. But the tradition represented by the Huguenot story is of tolerance which proceeds from conviction that it is God's will that we should show a tenderness towards the stranger and that we should be alert to the significance of the stranger as an agent of growth and enrichment. 'If God is for us, who is against us.'

It is a story to celebrate. It should not fuel complacency but should fortify our resolution to resist the strident voices of those who are heard in every age not least in ours, promoting the bigotry and racial animosity which would have made this country a less prosperous and altogether meaner place.

Opening of Parliament

> Wisdom is better than gold:
> Understanding is to be chosen rather than silver.[1]

PREACHING ON WHIT Sunday, just before the election, I made the point that whatever government should emerge, and whatever its policies and programmes, there was one thing we should all wish and pray for it – that it should prove a *competent* government. For it seems to me that a major task that falls to government, and a heavy burden that lies upon it, is that of responding competently and wisely to those unforeseen and unforeseeable crises and opportunities which constantly recur in the life of nations.

The great theologian Reinhold Niebuhr coined the phrase 'the cunning of history' to express the unpredictability of those twists and turns in human affairs which call for the attention and action of government. A government bemused and bewildered, reduced to panic or paralysis by the cunning of history comes very close to being no government at all. And a land without government becomes all too soon a land of sectional violence, no-go areas, kangaroo courts, and warring factions, with all their baleful consequences.

So I pray for this government,[2] and for the parliament from which it will receive both support and criticism, that they may both be blessed with wisdom. Expertise enables you to handle well what is predictable: only wisdom equips you to handle the unpredictable – to deal *competently* with whatever twist or turn of events may affect the life of the nation. Wisdom is a kind of flexible competence – a reserve of multi-purpose resources available for a multitude of eventualities. Wisdom signals balanced personality. Expertise in a narrow field can survive, even flourish in a person who is emotionally unstable or excited, or who is mentally or morally confused. But it is not in such a

---

[1] Proverbs 16.16.
[2] Sermon delivered at St Margaret's, Westminster, on 30 June 1987, on the occasion of the Opening of Parliament.

person that one expects to find wisdom. For this reason my prayer that you may be blessed with wisdom is much more than a piece of conventional politeness. For the wholeness of people who occupy such public positions as yours is increasingly threatened by the pressures of today.

I know myself something of these pressures – the pressure of living so much in the eye of the media that public image can become the puppet-master of private self; the pressure to give to public life more than can properly be spared by wife or husband or children, and to make so many acquaintances that there is no space left for friends. The pressure of receiving so much criticism which is arbitrary or unjust that one becomes impervious or resentful of *all* criticism.

These pressures bear upon all public figures: but upon you who exercise political power there fall in addition the deliberate impact of every lobby and pressure group, and the blandishments of the self-seeking flatterer. There is a Latin proverb which says, 'The first step of wisdom is to know what is false'.

Wise people are whole people, at one with the truth about themselves. The ways of the modern world assault that wholeness, and therefore the wisdom, of those who exercise political power. And so, what the world most needs of you, the world makes most difficult for you to retain. Therefore we owe to you, our democratically elected parliament and our legitimate government, a certain kind of quiet support. From all in the nation who pray, there is owed to you their prayer that you may be whole people. And there is owed from those who do *not* pray a thoughtful awareness that the possession of political power, enviable as it might seem from afar, discloses to a nearer view great and unavoidable strains upon the wholeness and integrity of its possessors.

This quiet support will seem most valuable to you if it meets within you a frank recognition of your need of support. I mean support more personal and intimate than the kind you have recently received from the electorate, and which you will receive from party colleagues. Each of you needs the support which will keep you together – for if you should crack or disintegrate, where shall wisdom be found in the debating chambers or the corridors of power?

I do not know from where, in the end, that support can come save from him 'in Whom we live and move and have our being'.

Opening of Parliament

'Let him that thinketh he standeth take heed lest he fall' wrote Paul. 'The frailty of man without Thee cannot but fall', says one of the beautiful collects in our Prayer Book. The mother and nurse of pride, said an ancient writer, is ignorance of God. Our Saviour has reminded us that of ourselves we cannot 'add one cubit to our stature': how much less can a few people aspire in their own strength to the wisdom to govern a nation?

You may remember that when King Solomon succeeded his father on the throne of Israel he prayed first and foremost for the gift of wisdom. He *prayed* – as one who knew not only that wisdom is necessary for good government, but also from what source wisdom comes. 'Where shall wisdom be found?' asks the Book of Job.[3] 'Where is the place of understanding? . . . Behold, the fear of the Lord – that is within; and to depart from evil is understanding'.

To pray for wisdom is not to expect or hope for direct and divine instructions over the handling of the nation's affairs. If it were it would be a dangerous and sinister practice, for no political leaders are so ruthless or so foolish as those who believe themselves to have a direct line to the Almighty. To pray for wisdom is to pray that, come what may, one may be held together as a person, with heart and head in balance, seeing oneself and others in just and proper proportion; knowing oneself, however eminent in the nation's life, to be still neither more nor less than the creature and child of God. To pray for wisdom is to pray that, despite all pressures and all temptations, one may become, and remain, a person for all seasons. I hope and trust that this will be your own private prayer, as well as the prayer of others on your behalf.

It is the heart of the Christian gospel, says St Paul, that 'In Christ all things hang together'. This was never more eloquently expressed than in these words of Martin Luther:

> From faith flows love and joy in the Lord, and from love, a joyful, willing and free mind that serves one's neighbour willingly, and takes no account of gratitude or ingratitude, praise or blame, gain or loss. As our heavenly Father has in Christ freely come to our help, we ought also freely to help our neighbour through our body and its works, and each should become as it were a Christ to the other, that we may be Christ to one another, and Christ may be the same in all.

[3] Job 28.12f.

One final point. To enter government or parliament for the first time must be a great moment, and to those whose moment has now come I wish you every joy. But for some – indeed for all – there must lie ahead, sooner or later, disappointments; situations in which you feel awkward, inadequate or out of place; times when you are overlooked for promotion or outstripped by contemporaries; matters over which you suffer painful criticism; occasions of great self-questioning and self-doubt. With every rise in status or power there rises more urgently the question of one's own identity, – 'Is this really me?', 'Do I really belong here?' I want to offer you the wise answer to these questions which Dietrich Bonhoeffer gave in a poem which he wrote in a Nazi concentration camp, not long before his execution. The poem is called 'Who am I?', and in it Bonhoeffer asks himself whether he really is what other people say and think he is. Looked up to by his fellow prisoners, held in awe even by the prison guards – is that the real Bonhoeffer? Or is he really what he knows of himself – a man just hanging on, lying awake at night in dread and loneliness and longing, nearly broken, almost in despair? Is that what he really is? Or is he something else again, a mass of contradictions, a confusion of opposites?

For a while Bonhoeffer can come to no answer, and the penultimate line of the poem is close to a surrender to despair: 'Who am I? They mock me these lonely questions of mine.' But then comes the final, decisive, triumphant line: 'Whoever I am, Thou knowest, O God, I am Thine.'[4]

Among the changes and chances of this world many people have found these words strengthening, even liberating. I hope that you who have to take on board so much at this time may nevertheless keep a space in your memory for this prayer against the time when you may need it: *'Whoever I am, Thou knowest, O God, I am Thine.'* Amen.

---

[4] Dietrich Bonhoeffer, *Letters and Papers from Prison* (SCM 1964), pp. 197-8.

Church and State

WHEN YOU FIRST invited me to accept your kind invitation to offer you some thought on the subject of Church and State, I expected that the national mood on the matter would, more or less as usual, be one of a rather disinterested complacency, punctuated by occasional rumblings of discontent and irritation. How wrong I was! Suddenly a storm blew up. Judging by my postbag and the media, the leadership of the Church has suddenly become the focus of excessive vituperation or extravagant praise. I find myself expected to give quick definitive answers to complex problems and to take on tasks, such as being an alternative ACAS, quite outside my competence. These are totally unrealistic expectations of the Archbishop of Canterbury.

Tonight,[1] I do not mean to dodge your questions – I will do my best with all of them. But, first, for a few minutes, I would like to step back from this turbulence and to seek a longer perspective on these events by looking for inspiration and insight from the presiding genius of your Club – Benjamin Disraeli.

At one point in *Tancred*,[2] which is, of course, a novel specifically about Church and State, Disraeli seems to have 1984 prophetically in mind when he writes:

> During our agitated age, when the principles of all institutions, sacred and secular, have been called in question; when, alike in the senate and the market-place, both the doctrine and the discipline of the Church have been impugned, its power assailed, its authority denied, the amount of its revenues investigated, their disposition criticised, and both attacked; not a voice has been raised by these mitred nullities either to warn or to vindicate; not a phrase has escaped their lips or their pens, that ever influenced public opinion, touched the heart of nations, or guided the conscience of a perplexed people. If they were ever heard of, it was that they had been pelted in a riot.

---

[1] Speech to the Coningsby Club in London, 24 October 1984.
[2] Disraeli, B. *Tancred*, first published 1847.

We have indeed seen bishops verbally pelted, but otherwise I feel that Disraeli, though he was penetrating about contemporary pressure on the Church, was incorrect about the silence of our bishops today.

So, failing to find inspiration from Disraeli I turned to Burke – only a small step backwards in Conservative thought, and a man who also held an exalted view of the Church's relation to the state. 'We will', he proclaimed in *Reflections on the French Revolution*,[3] 'have her to exalt her mitred front in courts and parliaments. We will have her mixed throughout the whole mass of life, and blended with all the classes of society.'

This triumphant view has a kind of romantic fascination about it, but of course it bears no relation at all to our present situation, nor do I believe, does it reflect the biblical understanding of the way in which God's Kingdom realizes itself in the visible world! So, I thought it might be revealing to search through two recent and well-known surveys of contemporary Britain to see what, if anything, is made of the Church/State connection.

The latest edition of Anthony Sampson's *Changing Anatomy of Britain*[4] was not helpful: he could not tell me much about the Church, for the only reference to it I could find concerned disestablishment. We have obviously become an unmentionable part of the nation's anatomy.

I also looked recently at the text of Ralf Dahrendorf's television lectures entitled *On Britain*.[5] Dahrendorf, the German born Director of the LSE, nowhere mentions the Church, but he does talk a very great deal about belonging, about solidarity, about community, and praises the way the British register these social attitudes and values. If he had probed a little deeper he would have realized that all these things spring from the vital tenacious and fundamentally *religious* roots of the nation. These values – loyalty, unity, interdependence and the sense of belonging are all about binding – the binding of individuals into a community and a United Kingdom. And 'binding', I should remind you, is the very root meaning of the word 'religion'. So I contend that these fundamental values, which, says Dahrendorf, hold us together as a nation, are values which take on meaning

---

[3] First published 1790.
[4] Hodder & Stoughton, 1982.
[5] University of Chicago Press, 1982.

and impetus from their specifically Christian origins. These values are still proclaimed by the established Church in a wide and pervasive way, though we are seldom given the credit.

I think the weaknesses of the Church can be exaggerated by those with a romantic view of its past or ignorance of its present life. Diminished in numbers and distanced from Westminster, it is still the largest network of voluntary associations for social well-being in the country. Time and time again it is this network, mostly staffed by the laity, that nudges the government with regard to care of the mentally handicapped, to overseas aid, to homelessness – to support higher standards of neighbourly concern and care. Above all the Churches still provide a nationwide meeting place for people of otherwise differing opinions to seek and find divine inspiration.

Some Anglicans, however, manifest a sense of guilt at having a privileged place in society, in government and education. They believe that Christianity is incompatible with intimacy with the rich and powerful. This is a question sharply relevant to those who sit in the House of Lords. Establishment-minded churchmen, we are told, enjoy the appearance of success, a success bought at the cost of reflecting the social values of their day. I disagree with that estimate of our position, because there is a difference between being relevant and merely being trendy. Bishops do not follow fashion. Our bishops in the House of Lords, after careful thought, quite often find themselves uneasy with, and sometimes plainly (though usually politely) hostile to the social values of the day; and neither do they give (nor are they expected to) unwavering loyalty to any one of the main political parties. They sit on the government side of the House since they believe in government as such. Order is itself the first freedom in a democratic society. But they are essentially crossbenchers, and they can and shall reflect the up-to-date feelings and opinions of the people in their dioceses.

There is one further argument of those who support disestablishment: they wish an end to the illusion – encouraged, they feel, by Establishment – that we are living in a Christian society. That is a point of view with which I have much more sympathy. Perhaps a streamlined Church, beholden only to the truth of its own teaching, would be better able to serve our Lord in the way he envisaged. But I believe this impossible. Many picture the pre-Constantine Church as a loosely knit association of charismatic groups of undogmatic leftist saints. It never existed – and we have to live the gospel in the world as it exists today. Human beings are influenced for good or ill not only by interpersonal relationships, but by important forces.

So, at present, I believe the achievement of disestablishment with its inevitably laborious legal ramifications, would waste years of precious Christian energy and might be more symbolically subversive to the Christian mission in England than continuing with the present arrangement.

Since 1919 the Church has been granted control over its own worship and doctrine, and a larger say in the appointment of its bishops. A partnership has evolved appropriate to the realities of the day in a typically British fashion. I will say no more about that now. But I believe it can work, though it cannot by being threatened and dissipated by extreme views on either side – those who would put the clock back to stricter Parliamentary control; those who would cut adrift and let synods rule.

Meanwhile many politicians exhort the clergy to concentrate on saving souls. Of course we are in the business of saving souls – but I am talking tonight about the social facet of a gospel which, as I said to the Salvation Army last week (in more high flown language than tonight, not suited to a Club Dinner), we believe Christ seeks to heal broken hearts, broken homes, broken bones and broken hopes.

My own attitude to a Church which attempts to offer society both a binding and a critique is summed up in the phrase 'critical solidarity'. That shall express the attitude of our Church to political authority. Solidarity is necessary because the task of government, whether central or local, in attempting to produce some tolerable realization of the common good amid so many conflicting interests is incredibly complicated. But *critical* solidarity is needed because the Church's task is more than that of providing a sacred canopy overarching the social order.

Thus I have sometimes vigorously supported the Government and its policies – over the Falklands, over many aspects of overseas aid; at other times over its determination to defeat terrorism, and in supporting general policies of multi-lateral disarmament. I have criticized the Government only when I have become convinced that certain policies are mistaken, or are being pursued in a manner inimical to the good of the whole community. This sort of criticism is usually about principles, sometimes about priorities. For example, last week, on behalf of the Synod, I accompanied a delegation to the Home Office to speak to the Home Secretary about the British Nationality Act. I believe that this Act and its rules continue to cause uneasiness, fears and insecurity both to individuals and to the community as a whole. Its operations can, I believe, be improved and I was pleased to find the present Home Secretary was not at all unsympathetic to our reasoned criticism, based on our wide first-hand experience.

As a further example, the week before last, during an interview published in *The Times*, I spoke of my concern at the long-term effects of unemployment. The Church's experience of unemployment is not limited to what a few bishops read in the newspapers. Up and down the country, the Church, often in co-operation with the Manpower Services Commission, but also on its own initiative, has set up and is running more than a hundred projects which offer some sort of new employment opportunities for those without work. I myself recently visited Creswell Colliery in Derbyshire, and heard at first hand of the fear which engulfs people when a coal-mine is threatened with closure. But I believe that fear has deeper roots than the purely local threat. It is the fear born of change over which people feel they have no control: technological change, the pulse of history, seems to be working against their whole way of life. Is this something a Christian Church should simply ignore? Is it something which can be assuaged by generous redundancy payments, or the promise of fresh work? It is not: it goes far, far deeper, and I think at last this will begin to be realized by those who are responsible for looking into our social and economic future. If we delay too long in recognizing we are in the midst of a long-term crisis about the nature and place of work in our contemporary society, then we shall find ourselves confronted by a generation of middle-aged anarchists, people totally without a sense of past achievement or hope for the future, who will vent their anger on the rest of us.

So what principles govern my interventions in political matters? I must emphasize that I speak for myself, and I do not speak as politician or diplomat, but I think that many bishops and clergy would find themselves in agreement with what I consider the ground rules for the discovery and articulation of our Christian response.

First, we need to unpack the moral principles involved in any issue. If we do this carefully we shall almost certainly reach down to the deeper currents flowing in the stream of history. A few years ago I was in the United States, where I met Robert McNamara. It was just after the publication of the Brandt Report, and he told me how he had recently been to Harvard to discuss its implications with the students there. He said that he had ignored the moral aspects of North/South economics and concentrated on the political and economic ones. When it came to the questions, he found himself roundly condemned for not having gone into the moral issues involved. I found that very encouraging. There are very few issues which do not have a moral dimension, and in sound Christian thinking a person's minding counts for just as much – and maybe more – as a person's mind.

Secondly, Christians must speak up for the poor and the powerless; the poor and the powerless both in body and spirit. Sometimes one might think that in the present climate the demonstration of compassion for the weakest in our society is some dangerous and subversive instinct. It is not. The protection of the weak is the first charge on a government's responsibilities.

The Welfare State, with all its problems and inadequacies, with all it can do to stifle individual effort, still represents a brave and far-reaching attempt to institutionalize Christian charity. It is a recent and remarkable achievement, and we should beware of excessive carping about its imperfections. There may be times when in building the nation we think more about ceilings than floors, but let us never forget that the house will not be fit for habitation or endure unless we give equal attention to both. When what the Bishop of Liverpool[6] called, in his Dimbleby Lecture, 'comfortable Britain' gradually slides into indifferent Britain, then we shall be sowing resentment, and we shall reap a bitter harvest. Our focus on the poor is a matter of attitudes as much as substance; a matter of communicating sympathy as much as raising benefits.

My third principle is designed to remind me that no country, and certainly not this one, is an island in more than the strictly geographical sense. Some of you will be far more knowledgeable than I am about the advance of the telecommunications industry.

---

[6] The Rt Rev. David Sheppard.

I think you will tell me that in the past ten years communications have been revolutionized, and doubtless the wider use of fibre optics and all kinds of computers will make the world yet smaller. My predecessors as archbishop, when they visited the outlying parts of the Anglican Communion, were away for months. I can do in hours what they did in days. The consequences of this are already immense: which of you does not study political happenings in the Gulf or South America with concern as great as your grandfathers reserved for events in the Balkans? I am daily made to realize that the Church, of which I am not the head but the focus of loyalty, is more black and brown and yellow than it is white. And that is how it should be, for Christianity, which itself was born at the crossroads between East and West, surely cannot be bound by ties of race or colour or creed, and, likewise, our moral concern should encompass the whole inhabited world – and that is, of course, literally what it means to be ecumenical. I suppose there is some kind of paradox in the fact that the established Church of England, with the monarch at its head, is one of the bodies most concerned to make us think internationally. The Queen, on all her travels and in her Christmas broadcasts, both as Head of the Commonwealth and Defender of the Faith, constantly reminds us that 'belonging' these days has an inescapable global perspective. I resist the idea that the Commonwealth is an abstract as I resist the idea that the Anglican Communion is an abstract; they both have equal gifts to give to the healing of a divided world.

My fourth principle underpinning everything I have said so far, is perhaps particularly Anglican: we appealed in the sixteenth century to Scripture, tradition and sound learning. I believe we have a responsibility to resist the mindless cults of unreason both in religious and political life: to strive for loyalty to truth, for sober, measured speech when so many people are shouting so loud that they have made themselves deaf. Self-righteous indignation is an opium which makes people unfit for useful work. Solzhenitsyn, one of my heroes, said enigmatically 'One word of Truth outweighs the world'. I believe that it is possible to marry together religious experience and faith in rational processes. A stone memorial to Dr Johnson, in a place where he liked to walk in North Wales, comments on his life and writings: 'He lent ardour to virtue and gave confidence to truth'. So if I go on complaining about megaphone diplomacy, it is because I believe much physical violence has its roots in the verbal violence pumped out by some politicians and journalists.

Those four principles: to look for the moral and spiritual dimensions of contemporary issues; to speak for the poor and powerless; to retain a global perspective; and to prefer reasoned argument and a respect for the truth to brute passion – these four principles guide my interventions in public affairs.

I should like to finish by giving you three assurances about Church and state in the future. The first is that the Church of England will continue by the grace of God to be faithful to the gospel we preach, and to be its defence in a questioning age. The second is that we shall continue in spiritual and human sympathy with those who have the arduous responsibility of the government of our nation. The third is that we shall continue to provoke the complacent and unsettle the somnolent. We may occasionally be turbulent priests, but we shall be turbulent because sometimes loyalty to Church and State makes silence impossible and criticism imperative. If we do this the caravan of Church and State will keep moving forward towards a future in which, by being faithful to our Church, we shall also bring enduring benefits to the State.

LIGHT – FOR THE WORLD

One Light for One World

IT IS APPROPRIATE that this ecumenical service[1] should take place in such a great and cosmopolitan city as Melbourne – a city where the Greek language in which St Paul wrote his letter to the Ephesians, is almost as widely spoken as English. Growing Christian unity cannot be isolated from growing unity within nations and between nations. The Churches' light should enlighten the world: 'One Light for One World' – the theme of our service.

Our reading from St Paul could scarcely give the preacher richer themes to explore the ecumenical pilgrimage: 'But grace was given to each of us according to the measure of Christ's gift . . . for building up the body of Christ, until we all attain to the unity of the faith and of the knowledge of the Son of God.'[2] St Paul shows that the Spirit of Christ bestows many gifts on his people to build unity in the body of Christ: one Spirit, many gifts, one body.

As I was preparing for my visit, I tried to brush up my Australian history. I pondered especially on the story of the Churches in Australia. I was struck by the immense variety and vitality of Christian expression and life in your country. From the beginning you have enjoyed a pattern of immigration which brought to this continent a wide spectrum of Christianity clothed in many historical and cultural forms. With the English came Anglicanism; with the Irish, Catholicism; the Welsh brought their Methodism; and the Scots their Presbyterianism. Central European immigration brought the Lutheran tradition. Since the Second World War further immigrations have added the Catholic and Orthodox cultures of southern Europe to this rich diversity. So, Australian Christianity is something of a unique ecumenical laboratory.

---

[1] Address at an Ecumenical Service in the Roman Catholic Cathedral of St Patrick, Melbourne, Australia, on 29 April 1985.
[2] Ephesians 4.7ff.

Each of these traditions inherited the European's identification of unity with uniformity, of oneness with sameness. Whatever the facts of history, the ideal remained 'one Church for one nation'. Anglicans in Australia now blush at early pretensions to establishment and the monopolization of education. Just 100 years ago, Church of England bishops in Australia could still object to 'Roman usurpations', or to 'State support of error' against Methodists or Presbyterians. Though I beat an Anglican breast we could all confess similar attitudes in the past. Thank God there is another thread running through your history: from competition to co-existence, from co-existence to co-operation. From co-operation we now aspire to communion.

St Paul speaks of a rich diversity of gifts. That the various Christian traditions have been blessed by God even in their separation is one of the fundamental insights of the ecumenical movement. It is because there is one Spirit revealed in an almost infinite variety of ways that we can begin to thank God not only for the gifts of our own Church, but also the gifts other Churches bring. Because the one Spirit is the author of the unique spiritual treasures of each Church, diversity can never be incompatible with unity.

The unity Christ wills must do justice to the profoundest insights of each Christian tradition. St Paul speaks of a mature unity in which all our differing gifts come together within the one body of Christ. It is this which reflects the fulness of Christ. I wonder: could the cultural mix of Australian Christianity prove to be a cradle for such a mature ecumenism in the future? Australian Christians could do worse than ask themselves what God is saying in setting so many precious traditions side by side.

I suppose I could be accused of succumbing to an Australian realism: live and let live. Differences don't matter. This is far from the truth. Both the New Testament and the early Christian tradition point to such a unity through which great diversity, even in fundamental expressions of our common faith, is allowed. Recent biblical scholars, common to all Churches, have suggested the gospel records are an amalgamation of what Jesus looked like to several different types of audience – that Jesus himself sought to bring God near to many groups in language which they could understand; that he accepted the various impressions of him this produced, but with a certain reserve towards all of them. We find different pictures of Jesus in different traditions. Mark gives us the strong Son of God; Matthew the giver of the new law; Luke the gentle friend of the poor and of sinners – to him alone we owe the stories of the Prodigal Son and the Good Samaritan; and in John we have the mysterious union of God and man. We cannot easily extract the Christ of Mark out of the Christ of John, or the Christ of Luke out of the Christ of Matthew. Yet we can see standing behind them all the one Christ to whom they all in the fellowship of the community strive to bear witness.

But let me add a word of warning. St Paul does not end with the Church. We are to attain 'unity in the faith' and 'mature *manhood*, to the measure of the stature of the fulness of Christ'. We follow a Lord who in his mission draws together like iron filings to a magnet the bits and pieces of a broken society. The friend of Roman, Greek and Jew; the teacher who thought up a provocative story about a good Samaritan heretic; the weekend guest of Pharisees who yet seemed to behave like a pagan on the Sabbath day; the intimate friend of women who were by no means all they ought to be. Among his disciples he numbered a publican and a Zealot. He was indifferent to custom as such – hostile to it when it built barriers between men. Yet who would describe him as merely tolerant? Here was the deepest commitment to God married to the most generous love for all his children.

Nothing less than the unity of the whole of humanity measures up to this 'fulness of Christ'. And, in the end, this is the point of our ecumenism. It must never become tamely ecclesiastical, absorbing our energies so that we fail to see that the unity of the Churches points beyond itself to the unity of the world. We must seek Christian unity not as a fearful coalition in headlong retreat from the secular world, rather we must seek it together to signal the wider unity of the whole human race in a divided and fragmented world – a world which so desperately needs the signs of God's reconciling love. 'One Light for One World' – this is our gospel.

In Australia, such Christian unity must speak with power to a young and vigorous nation made up of a great variety of cultures, and which must look increasingly to its role among its neighbours in Asia and Oceania. We must not lose sight of this wider context for Australian ecumenism in which St Paul's rich diversity of the gifts of the Spirit can take root and flourish and bring forth a rich and abundant harvest.

The Anglican Communion

A CHRISTIAN SYNOD is not so much a place for assertion but for listening and discovering.[1] We seek to know the will of God for his people, and that means listening not just to each other in the local situation but to the whole Church which has a wisdom and a breadth greater than any individual, group or nation. We in England may be justly proud that we have become the mother Church of a great Communion but we have to realize that today we are but one national church within a great partnership of autonomous churches. We take our place in what is arguably the second most widely distributed body of Christians. The Anglican Communion spans the world's races, cultures and social conditions; it represents an amazing diversity of human experience. All these local churches have much to learn from each other about what it means to be a Christian in today's world, and we in England have to extend our vision. We ignore what others have to teach us at our spiritual peril.

Coming as I do from Western Europe, where Christianity sometimes seems in retreat before a godless and restless materialism, I am delighted and heartened to discover that in many places, notably in Africa, Christianity is expanding and experiencing one of its great ages of mission. Today there are seventy million members of what is a growing Communion. There are now more black members than white and for a majority English is a second language. There is a lively and flourishing community of Anglicans in Japan with Japanese bishops and a Japanese primate. Latin America has scattered Anglican groups conducting their services in Spanish or Portuguese. In Africa and the Indian Ocean there are francophone dioceses. And, of course, the tiny community in Iran has given hope and inspiration to thousands around the world. Recent news items have reminded members of the Church of England that fellow Anglicans also include Palestinians.

---

[1] Presidential address to the General Synod of the Church of England, 21 November 1985.

One has only to think of Desmond Tutu's courageous witness in South Africa to realize that no longer are we a Church of the white middle-classes from the security and prosperity of the Western world, but we are also called to speak for Christ in places of poverty, injustice, alienation and persistent religious persecution. As I move in my travels and as I speak and correspond with the world's Anglican leaders I am sometimes overwhelmed both by the immensity of the tasks and by the richness of the opportunity.

At this point it would be tempting for me to become anecdotal about my recent visits around the Anglican Communion – but other people's travelogues are always trying and I do not want to encourage escapism from the immediate preoccupations of the Church of England. I want to say something about the Anglican Communion which is more than mere reminiscence and which will relate to the issues we shall be facing together in the next five years.

I believe it is of considerable significance that we call ourselves 'The Anglican Communion'. As Anglicans our identity is defined by communion rather than adherence to a confessional formula or subjection to an all pervading legal system. This is not to deny that Articles of Religion or canon law have their proper place. It is to affirm that the purpose of authority in the Church is to promote and maintain the Church's communion of life. The Churches' structures, such as the ordained ministry, must make possible a participation in the life of God and a sharing with each other. So Church authorities – even archbishops and General Synods – only exist to promote a vertical communion with God and a horizontal communion with the Church. This is what the first Epistle of John describes: 'That you also may have fellowship with us: and truly our fellowship is with the Father and with his Son Jesus Christ.'[2]

When Anglicans talk about 'dispersed authority' there is a temptation to think in facile, political terms – it can be used as a kind of democratic slogan. It is, rather, a theological principle of some profundity. Dispersed or shared authority is an authority which builds up the Church's fellowship with God and one another. Such authority is not to be understood as a diplomatic balance of power, of checks and balances, but as enabling the

---
[2] 1 John. 1.3.

people of God to share things in common at the most profound level.

When Anglicans speak of 'dispersed authority' they mean that there are many sources of authority, each of which has a claim to be heard. We have always given a unique place to the authority of holy Scripture; it is our proudest claim that we are a scripturally-based Church. The texts, though, have to be expounded and interpreted. We must listen to the traditional elucidations but also to those who bring to bear an honest, probing and responsible scholarship. We must respect the witness of tradition, the continuous teaching of a living Church, but we have to see it as dynamic: not the dead hand of the past but a way of taking essential Christianity into each new age. And we must take account of human Reason, not as a slavish following of contemporary intellectual fashions but rather as a principle of criticism of faith and action to establish moral priorities. But there are other sources of authority too which reside in particular people in particular situations. In Christian history the testimony of a confessor has always had greater weight than that of a mere scholar or administrator, and we ought to listen carefully to those who speak to us out of the sacrificial experience of living out the gospel in places of deprivation, conflict and despair. All these are sources of authority.

Another traditional Anglican view of authority has put together the Scriptures, the creeds, the Sacraments and the ordained ministry. These have become known, rather forbiddingly, as the 'Lambeth Quadrilateral'. This is not to be thought of as a kind of ecclesiastical 'check list' however. It is rather a description of the common life of the body of Christ. We share the gospel of God when the Scriptures are read. We share the faith of the Church when the creeds are recited. We share the life of the crucified and risen Christ when Baptism and the Eucharist are celebrated. And these 'holy things for the holy people' – as an Orthodox text puts it – are made possible by the ordered structure of the Church in the ordained ministry. Having this common life is what communion means. It is deeper than denominational and confessional trade-marks or loyalties to particular ecclesiastical constitutions. It is about the participation of human beings in God and in each other. And authority is to be the servant of such communion.

By serving a common Christian life at this basic level, authority actually gives us freedom for diversity at all other levels. Such an authority gives us space to be ourselves and to be different. It gives the Church liberty for radically divergent theologies, spiritualities, liturgies and disciplines. It gives a place for Catholic, Evangelical and liberal. It leaves room for dialogue, debate and even conflict. An authority which promotes and maintains the basic common life of the Church makes possible authentic Christian freedom. Its purpose is the 'Liberty of the children of God'.

In trying to outline some of the characteristics and spiritual principles of Anglicanism, I have also been elucidating the meaning of authority and communion. As I have said, I believe it is significant that we call ourselves a Communion. The reformed theologian, Lukas Fisher – a great ecumenist and one of the principal architects of the Baptism, Eucharist and Ministry agreement – once spoke of Anglicans 'almost accidentally rediscovering the Patristic principle of the communion of local Churches'. This does not always give us easy or immediate answers to problems. A communion of local churches does not possess a visible and instant magisterium. It therefore needs ways and occasions to gather these dispersed authorities. It has to work hard to develop what I can only describe as 'a sense of catholic solidarity': a belonging together, an interdependence, a sympathy, a love which forgoes pride.

While I believe it is right for us to be thankful for the providential pattern history has given us, we should not be complacent about the actual working out of authority and communion within the Anglican family. If communion – in the wide sense in which I have described – is to be maintained, we may need more effective links between the churches. These links exist in the Anglican Consultative Council, the Primates' Meeting, my own office as Archbishop of Canterbury and not least in the Lambeth Conference. But if we speak of strengthening international Anglican structures there will be some who will want to counter by emphasizing the National Sovereignty and Independence of the Church of England. To this I would reply that while Anglican Councils have properly been called 'Bonds of Affection', it is also true that from the time of the first Lambeth Conference affection took structural form in order that the communion of life between the Churches should be maintained. Had Anglicans possessed a stronger sense of communion expressed in a more structured affection just a few years ago, it is arguable that we might have handled the question of the ordination of women in a more satisfactory way. Nor should we ignore the symbolic role of the bishop, both as the local focus of unity and the link of communion between his church and the wider Church. Every bishop has a responsibility for the universal Church though some bishops historically have a more specific and wider responsibility. Episcopacy and primacy are there to foster shared responsibility for communion.

Perhaps this is the moment to speak of how I understand my own role within the Anglican Communion. It is clear that the mass media would sometimes like to treat me as the Anglican equivalent of the Pope; they find it easier to concentrate their attention on a person rather than a committee, especially when that person lives in a sophisticated modern capital with a diplomatic network and efficient communications. There is, therefore, a constant demand for crisis management, for pronouncements from someone whom they can identify as an authority figure. I should like to assure you that I am aware of the dangers in this. The Archbishop of Canterbury is the senior bishop of the whole Communion and his see has a historic relationship to all the others, but he is still one bishop among many, and his role is fraternal not papal. He is the eldest brother in a family but the other members are mature, independent and equal in status. So his role is to gather the Churches, not to rule them. In fact, my response to Bishop Desmond Tutu's appeal for support in sending the Bishop of Lichfield to attend the recent tragic funeral in South Africa speaks more eloquently about episcopacy and primacy, interdependence, collegiality and communion than any debate in this Assembly Hall.

Likewise I hope that Bishop Keith Sutton's visit will help the Church of England to see something of the universal horizons and responsibilities Communion imposes upon bishops, not least Archbishops of Canterbury. The office of the Archbishop of Canterbury is something the Church of England can offer to the Anglican Communion. Of course, the availability of my office to the Communion will be at a cost to the Church of England, that is what communion is all about. But communion is also always reciprocal. Other Anglicans have a deep affection and sense of responsibility for the Church of England. Let us not be too independent to receive affection and admonition in return.

This brings me to the Lambeth Conference. In inviting the bishops to the 1988 Lambeth Conference I have asked each bishop 'to bring his diocese with him'. If the Lambeth Conference is not to be simply another episcopal meeting, it is essential that the themes of the conference are studied and discussed in the local Church prior to Lambeth and followed up by the local Church afterwards. Only if this happens will the bishop be the link between the local and the universal of which I have spoken.

The conference will consider a range of issues under four general headings: Mission and Ministry; Matters Doctrinal and Pastoral; Ecumenical Relations; and Christianity and the Social Order. Some of these involve matters which divide Anglicans, not least the continuing debate about the ordination of women, and we shall be looking for understanding and reconciliation among ourselves.

I have to say, however, that I think it would be a complete failure of vision if we spent overmuch time on the identity and coherence of Anglicanism. We shall be dealing with urgent questions which face all mankind and we must act as serious religious people who believe that Christ and the Gospel can make all the difference to a world full of hopelessness, violence and want. We are bearers of our Lord's promise to save and renew our humanity. It is essential that we do not produce statements which are trivial or couched in a religious jargon which the world cannot understand. When we discuss matters of mission and ministry we must be heard to be the bearers of real good news and to be restoring individuals and societies to peace and health. On dogmatic and pastoral questions we must be seen to be battling seriously for the truth of the Christian faith and for its coherence. In our work on ecumenical relations we need to realize that in many parts of the world Christian unity is not a luxury but an urgent necessity for credible mission and the unity of peoples. In our debates on Christianity and the social order we have to clarify our thought about war, the family and social justice, for the world looks for action and involvement by Christians, not pious words from the side-lines. Having said this I will not bore you with the details of the agendas of each section, but I would like to underscore some of the issues which will be of special concern to us in England.

Our cities have recently become the focus of national and international attention. Handsworth, Tottenham and Brixton are now known in Delhi and San Diego. The report of my Urban Priorities Commission[3] will shortly be published and it will have much that is significant to say about the role of the Church in the city. This is the sort of issue which will come fairly and squarely before the Mission and Ministry section of Lambeth, though the scale will of course be global.

The Doctrinal and Pastoral section will have before it the report of the Inter-Anglican Theological and Doctrinal Commission, to be published early next year. Among its themes is the relation between faith and culture, not irrelevant to England's multi-racial and multi-cultural society.

This will also be the section in which the Church of England's own doctrinal debate will have its place. I hope the Lambeth Conference will be able to say something about the bishop's collegial responsibility for doctrinal discernment, judgement and articulation. The work of the House of Bishops and the response of the General Synod will be an important part of this discussion.

Ecumenical relations will put BEM[4] and ARCIC[5] before the Lambeth Conference for a definitive evaluation in the light of synodical responses throughout the world. If BEM is endorsed by the Anglican Communion it will offer just the kind of firm doctrinal foundation which was felt to be lacking in the Covenant proposals and could provide the basis for new ecumenical relationships. An endorsement of ARCIC, especially on the Eucharist and Ministry, would be of crucial significance for Anglican/Roman Catholic relations. Acceptance of the Eucharist and Ministry statements would now provide a new context for the recognition of ministries. I need not spell out what an immense step forward that would be.

The Church of England will also be much involved in the fourth section of the Lambeth Conference, Christianity and the Social Order. Our debate about Church and Politics will be part of its agenda. But personal ethics will also play a major part in the debate. An international study of the family is being planned and preparation of this will involve co-ordination with the Anglican Church in Australia.

I hope I have said enough to show that the themes of the

---

[3] Published 3 December 1985.
[4] Baptism, Eucharist and Ministry. Faith and Order Paper No. 111 of the World Council of Churches, Geneva.
[5] Final Report of the Anglican-Roman Catholic International Commission.

conference are live issues for the Church of England. Dioceses and General Synod can have a real part to play before 1988 so that the bishops authentically represent the thought and convictions of their churches. Communion, as I have said, means sharing. This means bringing the things that matter in the local church to the attention and judgement of the wider Church. It also involves bringing the discussion back from Lambeth to the local church. The Lambeth Conference can thus be an instrument for the living Communion I have been describing. What authority the Lambeth Conference possesses will serve that living Communion, and the conference will be a means by which our Anglican family becomes what it claims to be – an Anglican Communion.

We know that we do not meet in Synod simply in order to have enjoyable debates, or to gain personal distinction, or to promote our own policies and ideas. We meet and work for the good of large constituencies in this country in order to strengthen and advance Christian influence in those constituencies.

I have given this address with one aim in mind. That we shall show an understanding during the next five years that our commitment to world mission will be more specific and focused if we have an understanding of the resources, the character and the particular vocation of the Anglican Communion.

Enthronement in Uganda

A PRAYER OF the Apostle Paul for the Church in Rome: 'May God, the source of patience and encouragement, enable you to have the same point of view among yourselves by following the example of Christ Jesus, so that all of you together may praise with one voice the God and Father of our Lord Jesus Christ.'[1]

This glorious service of enthronement[2] is a vision of the fulfilment of that heartfelt longing of St Paul. Here, for a time, are gathered archbishops and bishops, clergy and laity from our own Anglican Church and from other Churches, from every region and tribe of Uganda as well as from other parts of Africa, and still further afield from the United States and Canada and England. All this rich variety of people is together, united in Christ Jesus, praising with one voice the God and Father of us all. Surely, the Lord is here, his Spirit is with us!

Such a gathering as this, such vision, marks a whole new start, a new chapter in the history of the Church and the nation of Uganda. Here begins a new life not only for our brother Yona, your new archbishop; not only for his province and its dioceses and parishes and people. Here too is the hope of a new start for all the people of this beautiful country of whatever church or religion, or of none. An archbishop is enthroned for a life of service and dedication, not only to the people of his own Church, but to all the people of his society. He is there to witness to all how every human being should live and love.

Of all the nations of the earth, you deserve a new beginning. The world has not been deaf to the stricken cries of the people of Uganda – we have heard the screams of a people subjected to appalling suffering at the hands of cruel and godless men. Perhaps it is impertinent of me to speak of what you have had to endure, and yet the past is something we cannot and should not

[1] Romans 15.5f.
[2] Of the Rt Rev. Yona Okoth as Archbishop of Uganda, in the Provincial Cathedral of Namirembe, Kampala, on Sunday 29 January 1984, when the Archbishop of Canterbury preached.

forget. As you stand on the threshold of a new hope, you do well to recall the long, hard road that has brought you here. In these dark years you have suffered the violation of every human right. Your country has been ravaged by torture and murder and atrocities of every kind. You have been subjected to poverty, hunger, disease, imprisonment and homelessness. You have been driven to terror and despair by the tyranny of ruthless and inhuman oppression; Church and nation alike have suffered the cruelest persecution. And from the tumult of this persecution, the cries of one victim above all have echoed across the world. I speak, of course, of our brother Archbishop Janani Luwum, murdered as, in obedience to Christ and in service to his people, he stood up to protest against injustice, brutality and tyranny. The death of Janani was nothing less than a martyrdom. His death is a living witness to the power and courage of Jesus Christ himself, revealed above all in his suffering love on the cross.

The wonder and power of martyrdom is something I am never allowed to forget in Canterbury. There, today, our great and marvellous cathedral, the mother church of our Anglican Communion, stands as a permanent reminder of one of my own predecessors, Archbishop Thomas Becket. He was brutally murdered himself some 800 years ago as a result of another violent collision between Church and State, archbishop and ruler; but the blood of the martyrs is the seed of the Church,[3] and from that desolate moment of death and despair sprang a deep devotion in England and with it an invigorated faith in our Lord Jesus Christ. Canterbury Cathedral, the site of Becket's death, was soon enlarged and enhanced to make it a fitting and holy place for the martyr's shrine.

Today, at the eastern end of the Cathedral, just beyond the site of Becket's shrine, stands the Chapel of 20th Century Martyrs. Archbishop Luwum is not only one of the martyrs commemorated there – the very idea for such a chapel was inspired by his death. Present, too, in this Chapel is a beautiful and moving statue of 'The Burial of Christ' by Rosemary Namuli, who studied here at Makerere University. It depicts the body of Christ, wrapped in a bark cloth, being carried to the grave as in a Muganda funeral. To today's millions of pilgrims and sightseers, it is a vivid reminder not only of Uganda but of what Christian martyrdom is about –

[3] Tertullian, *Apologeticus* 50.13.

the sharing in the very suffering and death of Christ himself and in his life-giving victory. That is why Christians are so excited by martyrdom, that is why it gives us such hope. You know better than most, from the noble beginnings of the churches in this land, that: 'The blood of thy martyrs and saints shall enrich the earth and create the holy places.' Out of the blood of martyrdom springs a vigorous church.

Every Ugandan, here and elsewhere, has shared in the sufferings of Christ – whether they know it or not. But Christians are those who know that to share in Christ's agony and death is to share too in his joy and risen life. It is your life in Christ, your life as brothers and sisters of Jesus, which you must reveal to those around you. Living out Christ's own life means following his example, it means becoming more and more Christ-like. Above all it means loving, loving with all the inexhaustible energy of Christ's own love. Christ's love was not confined to his family and friends and compatriots. Jesus' love extended even to those who hated him and plotted against him and had him scourged and crucified. 'Love your enemies', he said, 'and pray for those who persecute you.' This is the love which must flow from your new archbishop and from your bishops and clergy, and from each and every Christian. This is the love which will make others sit up and take note. This is the love which can bind up your wounds and bring healing and hope.

'Father forgive them – they know not what they do.' So prayed Jesus for those who put him to death. Such a prayer as this, such remarkable powers of forgiveness, seem beyond us. And yet Christ's way is the way of pardon, mercy and reconciliation – it is never the stony path of revenge, retaliation and burning hatred. The Christian must settle old scores not with the gun but with the olive branch. Once again, this is an example which Yona must set – he is your supreme 'bridge-builder'. But it is Christ's own example, and must be followed by everyone who calls himself a Christian.

Christ came not to be served, but to serve, and it is in selfless and humble service of others that we follow Christ, our master. Yona is here to be enthroned, but the throne of an archbishop is not the throne of a king or a paramount chief; it does not invest him with political power and force of arms. An archbishop's throne is Christ's own throne – the symbol of a very different authority – the authority of obedience, self-sacrifice and service;

the power of one who stoops to wash his disciples' feet. Though today Yona is made an archbishop, he remains also a deacon, a servant, one 'entrusted with the ministry of Jesus Christ himself'.[4] I pray that the trappings and temptations of the power and authority of the world will never entice Yona away from the true power of Christ. It is with that power that he must care for and encourage and wait upon his fellow bishops, and it is with this same power again that they must serve their clergy, and so it goes on as one brother or sister of Christ serves another. 'Among you, whoever wants to be great must be your servant, and whoever wants to be first must be the willing slave of all.'[5]

Brothers and sisters of Christ, united in love, forgiveness and service, are together children of the same heavenly Father. And it is perhaps in developing and strengthening your unity as Christians, a unity that must cut right across your denominational, political and tribal differences, that Christians can be of the greatest service to the whole people of Uganda in the years ahead: 'We are the Body of Christ. In the one Spirit we were all baptized into one body. Let us then pursue all that makes for peace and builds up our common life.'

Within our Anglican province of Uganda I hope that Archbishop Yona will travel widely, extending to every diocese a strong sense of belonging to one Anglican fellowship. It is for the bishops and the dioceses also to think above and beyond regional and ethnic boundaries to the church of this province, embodied in your new archbishop. You must trust one another; you must be loyal to one another; you must love, forgive and care for one another. 'There must be no room for rivalry and personal vanity among you, but you must humbly reckon others better than yourselves. Look to each other's interest and not merely to your own. Let your bearing towards one another arise out of your life in Christ Jesus'.[6]

Charity begins at home, but it must not stay there – it must extend to other Churches with which you share so much in suffering and success. Great strides are being made across the world to foster a growing love between Anglicans and Roman Catholics. On a marvellous, even miraculous occasion eighteen

---

[4] Ignatius of Antioch, Epistle to the Magnesians.
[5] Matthew 20.26–7.
[6] Philippians 2.3f.

months ago, His Holiness Pope John Paul II accompanied by Cardinal Nsubuga, whom I met again yesterday, made a pilgrimage to Canterbury. At an historic service in the Cathedral we knelt side by side in prayer to the one God and Father of us all. We affirmed our common faith and renewed our baptismal vows, and at the height of the service we walked together to the Martyrs' Chapel. There we remembered with gratitude Archbishop Janani, and we were reminded of our one faith in Christ who died to save us all. I said then that:

> If we remember that beginning in Jesus Christ our Lord, if we can face the suffering involved in travelling his way, if we can lift our eyes beyond the historic quarrels which have tragically disfigured Christ's Church and wasted so much Christian energy, then we shall indeed enter a faith worthy of celebration because it is able to re-make the world.

Such love and unity between Christians, which overcomes the world's divisions, can indeed transform our world and re-make this nation. If, together, Christians in this land would stretch across the chasms which separate, and take hold of the hand of fellowship, what powerful witness that would be to all your people! The road to unity and co-operation will be hard and costly, but it will point the way forward for your whole nation; it will show just what is possible for your people. It is for each and every Christian to testify to the world that in Christ Jesus we are all children of our Father in heaven. That is the most important truth of all, and it is by witnessing to this gospel that Christians here can ensure that Uganda will rise again!

A New Presiding Bishop

THIS CONVENTION[1] HAS special significance, for this is the month in which we celebrate the bicentenary of the first General Convention. That small gathering in Philadelphia in September 1785 met when the very *survival* of Anglicanism in the United States was in doubt. Amid the turmoil of revolution, the old Church of England in the American colonies had been shattered, and many of its clergy had fled. The Philadelphia Convention was composed of clergy and laity who had supported the revolutionary cause. They set to work to fashion an independent church in an independent nation. Led by the brilliant young William White of Pennsylvania, they sought to re-form the Church with the democratic ideas of their new republic. So, in the 'Philadelphia plan' the Episcopal Church was to be independent of any outside authority and responsible for its own doctrine, canons and liturgy. The dioceses were to be federated under the triennial general convention. Bishops were to be elected officers working under a constitution, and the laity were to have equal voice with the clergy.

It was a scheme which accorded well with the aspirations of the independent United States, and its basic wisdom has been shown by the way it has become a model for other independent Anglican churches. But it was right for Samuel Seabury of Connecticut, then the only American bishop, to sound a note of warning. He refused to attend the Convention until the authority of bishops as guardians of the faith of the whole Catholic Church had been safeguarded. He feared that Enlightenment philosophy might separate the Convention from the body of Catholic Christianity. The proposed constitution, he protested, would 'bring the clergy into abject bondage to the laity'. 'A bishop', he said, 'has no more power in the Church than a lay member. Doctrine, Discipline, Liturgies are all to be under lay control.'

[1] Address at the Opening Service of the 68th General Convention of the Episcopal Church of the United States of America, at the Anaheim Convention Centre, California, 8 September 1985.

When the Convention began to revise the wording of the creeds his worst fears were fulfilled, and there was danger of *two* Episcopal Churches. You will not mind my reminding you that the tension was eased by the counsel of the Archbishop of Canterbury. The changes in the creeds were withdrawn and in 1786 William White and Samuel Prevoost were consecrated bishops in the chapel of Lambeth Palace. A sound Anglican compromise was reached by the creation of a separate House of Bishops in the General Convention of 1789.

To turn to the present and this important time in your history. At this Convention – in historic continuity with that convention 200 years ago – you are to elect a new Presiding Bishop who will guide you as you confront the many problems and opportunities of your Church in today's world. I have found myself wondering what St Paul would say were he writing a letter to this Convention. He would, I am sure, address you on some aspect of the building up of the body of Christ.

Here the need for balance between the local and universal dimensions of the Church is paramount, and is something which is now felt in all the great international Christian communions. It finds its roots in the kind of commission given in the sixth century by Pope Gregory to my first predecessor, St Augustine. Preach the gospel, he said, but be sure to preserve the local customs and traditions. This was sound advice for it is essential that there should be expressions of Christian faith and community which are grounded in particular cultures, societies and economies. The gospel is often most powerfully preached when it is related to a people's search for identity, justice and freedom.

Such local expressions of the Church, however, can be limited in sympathy and partial in understanding. The Church is unavoidably conformed to the culture in which it is set and to which it must preach, and it is all too easy to identify the spirit of the age with the spirit of God. We have now come to recognize the insensitivity of much of the nineteenth century missionary movement with its disregard of ancient African and Asian ways of life. We exported too much Englishness with the gospel, and Christianity must have had all the appearance of a foreign religion. The Christian Church exists in many different cultures, and the gospel is proclaimed with the aid of many different philosophies, but it is not to be *identified* with any of them. Ours is a world in which the speed of modern communication has created a 'global village', and with a sense of common humanity with common fears, needs, strivings and hopes.

For the Churches that means discovering what is a legitimate and lifegiving diversity. It also means never losing sight of that common positive catholic faith which all Christian Churches share. In the early Church there were wide differences in theology and usage but there was a strong sense of common tradition which kept the Churches together in unity and mission. Today that means listening not just to other members of our own communion but to the voice of the ecumenical movement as it tries to move beyond merely denominational positions. An international fellowship of Churches is more likely to be self-correcting than one that never looks beyond its own boundaries.

Our Anglican Communion shares both the tension and the hope. We have developed into a world-wide family of Churches. Today there are seventy million members of what is arguably the second most widely distributed body of Christians. No longer are we identified by having some kind of English heritage. For a majority of our members, English is a second language. There are more black members than white. Our local diversities span the spectrum of the world's races, needs and aspirations. We have only to think of Bishop Tutu's courageous witness in South Africa to be reminded that we are no longer a Church of the white middle classes allied only to the prosperous Western world.

Amid such a diversity how do we come to a common mind? We possess no rigid confessional basis, nor have we the kind of *magisterium* which solves our problems by pre-emptive pronouncement. History has set the see of Canterbury at the centre of our Anglican unity, but its role is to gather the family not to rule it. The power to decide in matters of faith, order and morals remains with the local church. This could so easily be a recipe for incoherence and for that ecclesiastical isolationism which pays scant regard to the convictions of others. Much therefore depends on what I can only describe as 'a sense of Catholic solidarity'.

The wisdom and love of Christ are *given* to us. It is not the mark of a Christian to be for ever asserting personal opinions. Within the community of faith we listen, share and are deepened and opened to the will of God, and are changed into his likeness. In the end, we belong to the whole catholic Church of God which has a breadth and an enduring strength greater than that of any individual or particular church. It is this 'sense of solidarity' which has allowed the Church through the ages to deal with great questions in order to get on with its chief task of witness, mission and service.

I believe that in three years time we shall be tested as to whether we can put this ideal into practice. Preparation is under way for the Lambeth Conference in 1988. We have already begun work on the major issues to be considered, so that each bishop can share them with his diocese and root them in their particular situation. When the bishops come to Lambeth they will not then come as private individuals. They will bring their dioceses with them. So each bishop will fulfil the true role of a bishop in the Church of God: he will represent the local church, but he will also be a part of an episcopal college which has a care for all the churches.

The conference will be asked to consider a range of pressing issues under four sections: Mission and Ministry; Matters Doctrinal and Pastoral; Ecumenical Relations and Christianity and Social Order. That is a very broad agenda. It will need careful discipline. We shall be dealing with matters which divide Anglicans but we shall be looking for understanding and for reconciliation. Yet it would be failure of vision merely to be concerned with the identity and coherence of the Anglican Communion. There are issues which face the whole Church as we seek to preach Christ and gather men and women into a community which is itself called to be a promise of a new humanity. In a world full of despair, violence, injustice and want, we must seek to renew the preaching of the gospel, to reform the structures of the Church, and to redirect our minds and our lives to the task of loving and serving those in need, powerlessness and alienation. The Lambeth Conference will, we hope, point the way forward for our part of the whole catholic Church. If it is to bear this kind of fruit it will need the contributions of this convention – not least your prayers, your reflections, and in particular your strong sense of history combined with a creative readiness to serve the future.

Let me finish on a personal note. When sometimes I stand in the silence and stillness of the great cathedral at Canterbury, I reflect that so far from everything being at peace, I am surrounded by mighty forces. The high vaults are striving to push the walls outwards; the buttresses are trying to push them inwards; the aisle vaults are doing their best to push the nave columns inwards but are unable to move them under the weight of the triforium. The whole fabric is struggling to explode and come crashing down. Yet forces which could prove so disastrous and destructive are miraculously harnessed into a building of transcendent and indescribable beauty and harmony.

Within the construction of our Church, within the building up of the body, there are today many countervailing forces which make for destruction and disintegration. But our faith and trust is in One who can take us and build us up into a rich and various solidarity and unity which may be used in his service and to his honour and glory in the years to come. Amen.

Mission and Evangelism

> Go forth and make all nations my disciples, baptise men everywhere ... and teach them to observe all that I have commanded you.

THE MARAMON CONVENTION[1] and the local conventions which have been taking place recently, are reminders to us that Christianity is a missionary religion. Here, with Jesus' great commission, St Matthew brings his Gospel to an end. This final command to his followers marks the climax of all that Jesus said and did to bring life, hope and healing to the world. Here is our common call today to mission, to evangelism, to go out and commend the gospel.

I am aware that as I speak here in Kerala, I am speaking on missionary soil where (tradition has it) St Thomas first brought the gospel to India. I am aware that many of you are descendants from those first Christians. I am also aware that I am an apostolic successor of St Augustine, the first missionary Archbishop of Canterbury who brought the gospel to England. It is appropriate that the successor of a missionary saint should be talking to the successors of another missionary saint about the mission of the Church.

Sharing the gospel is essential – because Jesus commands it, and because *without* evangelism the gospel would soon become no more than a relic from a forgotten history. Without our mission, the Christian Church would become one more human institution which had outlived its relevance and its usefulness. So in spite of the *history* of mission in both our traditions it is crucial that we channel our Christian energies into preparing for the *future*, into ensuring that we have a vital and vigorous Church to hand on to those who come after us.

It was to ensure a new vitality within your Church, a new awareness of mission, that the first mission of help was sent to

---

[1] Address to the annual Maramon Convention of the Mar Thoma Church, Kottayam, Kerala, South India, Sunday 23 February 1986.

you from my Church. From that time on and from the period of Reformation in the Mar Thoma Church, Anglicans and Mar Thoma Christians have continued to support each other in the proclamation of the gospel. These are links which I value enormously, though I am the first to admit the shortcomings as well as the strengths of our common history. There was too much of the imperial thought in those early acts of missionary enterprise. There was, to begin with, too much export of Englishness alongside the proper sharing of the gospel.

That was surely *not* what Jesus intended when he commanded his disciples to make followers of every nation. Your continued loyalty to the tradition of St Thomas is an important witness to the fact that the gospel has to be planted in each nation in a way such as to preserve intact its culture and customs. The gospel must be at home and in touch with the place and people where it has taken root. Christ must have here an authentic Indian face, and this is something I am deeply thankful for in the Mar Thoma Church.

But *how* do we approach our task of evangelism? What are the methods we should employ? I want to mention three. They are not mine and they are not new. They are three well-tried and tested ways which are central to our Christian faith because they are ways which come first and foremost from our Lord himself.

First: 'Faith comes from what is heard', says St Paul, 'and what is heard comes by the preaching of Christ'. The faithful proclamation of the Gospel, Sunday by Sunday, in the services of the Church, this is the source of Christian faith, as well as its continuing nourishment. It is here that the Word of God to his people is made plain, so that those with ears to hear will hear. In this way, the good news of the life, death and resurrection of our Lord Jesus Christ can be set before people with all its glory and wonder.

We live today in an age of rapid and aggressive communication. Modern technology, simplistic sloganizing, instant appeal, all these encourage a form of proclamation whose clamour can contradict and undermine the very gospel of peace and patience which it claims to preach. In the face of crude and dogmatic evangelism we need to stand firm and combine the virtues of conviction and enthusiasm for the gospel with reasonable thought and attention.

The presbyter or minister whose sermons and services are

both passionate and sober can be an effective 'bridge-builder' between Christians and those who follow different faiths. He is a man who listens and understands, while his own beliefs are never in doubt. He can help the Christian to revere the wisdom and beauty of other religions, and he can help their followers to recognize the love and truth of the hidden Christ.

But it would be a mistake to look only to our bishops and presbyters to see our bridge-builders. The Christian Church has a priesthood of all believers. Every Christian is called to the task of evangelism and the making of disciples. It may not be every Christian's vocation to preach from the pulpit, but it *is* every Christian's task to gossip the gospel. We need to be willing to talk about our faith and our life in Christ when the opportunity arises – at home, at work, at school, or wherever. Here, it is the layman who has all the opportunities for outreach.

It is always tempting for the Church to retreat into an inward-looking ghetto, into what is sometimes a self-satisfied holy huddle. It would be easy to be carried away by the words of a convention speaker, to be enthusiastic about the gospel but do nothing about taking it to others. So, it is essential that we seize what God-given chances we have to speak up for what we believe in, and to share with others the good news of God's love. On his return home to England, not so long ago, a missionary had this to say: 'One of the worst attitudes in the Christian life is enjoying the benefits of salvation and keeping the knowledge to oneself. In the desert, the greatest of all crimes is that of knowing where the water is, and keeping the knowledge to yourself.'

And people need to *see* the gospel and not just hear it. Seeing is believing, and actions can often speak louder than words. As well as preaching and gossiping the gospel, we must actually *live* the gospel. We must put our faith into practice. I am convinced that this is where the most effective evangelism takes place – through people seeing in others the true wonder and quality of Christian life: life which abounds with love, joy, patience, kindness and goodness. It means compassion and care for those who suffer: the diseased and dying, the destitute and despised. In India I have already seen many moving and impressive examples of deep Christian care: on the streets of Bombay, in the marvellous work of Mother Teresa in Calcutta, in the Christian Medical Service in Vellore. In the Mar Thoma Church you have a good tradition of care for the deprived and the poor begun by Metropolitan Mar

Juhanon and continued under Metropolitan Alexander. But living the gospel is more than simply supporting institutions – essential as this is.

There is a British saying that 'charity begins at home'. It is a good saying providing it is not taken to mean that charity must begin and end at home. But Christian witness does indeed begin in our own homes – and that is often much harder than we might think. I am sure you have family prayers each morning and evening, but has this just become a formal family routine presided over by the father of the family, or is it a relaxed time together when the family can say what the Scriptures are saying to them and share each other's problems and prayers? Is it a time when the family tries to understand what God is saying to them?

If you have servants, do you treat them as you would your own children – for that is how God loves you. Are they so touched by the quality of your life that they ask you about your Christian faith? And how do your own children respond to the Christian gospel? Do they see it as giving them the freedom to grow up as God intends them to be?

A Christian employer has a responsibility in setting good moral business standards and in caring for his staff and their families. A Christian employee must also serve willingly and honestly. The first Christians were distinctive – they were different to other people – because they had a special joy. India is a country of many religions – are the Christians distinctive because of their joy?

We also need too to show the world the love and unity which exists between Christians both within our parish and diocese, and between Christians of different Churches and traditions. Division and antagonism between Christian brothers and sisters is a prime cause of the Church's failure to speak clearly of the love of Christ. Preaching love without putting love into practice is at best a wasted effort, and at worst an hypocrisy which impedes and imperils the building of God's kingdom.

The Mar Thoma Church already has a good record for working towards Christian unity – again going back to Metropolitan Mar Juhanon. You are in communion with the Anglican Communion, you are seeking a close unity with the Churches of North and South India through your joint council. This *is* related to your mission. The world will hardly believe the Christian gospel of reconciliation if the Churches themselves remain unreconciled.

The mission of the Church in India has its own particular problems. Kerala is called 'the land of coconuts and bishops' and I have seen plenty of both! In Kerala there are many Churches – some of the divisions are now historical, others were imported by missionaries, but Jesus prayed: 'May they all be one – so that the world may believe that you sent me.'[2] A divided Church is a poor missionary Church. Jesus does not pray that we should be united because he liked large organizations; he prayed that we might be one 'so that the world may believe'. Our search for Christian unity is linked with the missionary role of the Church.

India is described as 'the land of many religions' and all of you will know good people of other faiths. I recognize that many Hindus have a love for Christ but feel unable to become Christians. People of many faiths have much in common and I am sure that we must learn to work together and to talk together. We need to be a serving Church and a listening Church. At the heart of Jesus' own ministry and prayer is his longing and his desire that they may all be one. It is in this prayer and ministry that we are called together: 'Go forth therefore and make all nations my disciples . . . and be assured I am with you always, to the end of time.'[3] Amen.

---

[2] John 18.21.
[3] Matthew 28.19–20.

ARCIC and Authority

I SPOKE EARLIER in this Synod of my recent visit to Assisi as well as to Switzerland. So far we have had some quality theology in this debate and some substantial history. I want to be rather personal, circulating round the two major principles at stake.[1]

First, our conversations with Rome remind us of the universality of the Church. Whether we like it or not, there is only one Christian Church, only one bishop who could have effectively convoked such an ecumenical spectrum of Christian leaders as met at Assisi – Baptists and Orthodox, Reformed and Quakers, Methodists and Lutherans, Orientals and Anglicans, as well as the Roman Catholic Church itself. That is one of the reasons why I have, in a modest way, encouraged the Pope, ever since we talked at Canterbury, about the idea of bringing together a religious day of prayer for peace. Rome has certain historical roles which simply cannot be ignored, however we wish to evaluate them theologically. And when we look at the other great world religions, it is a fact that our inter-Christian squabbles seem less significant. The other great communities of faith regard the Pope as somehow the main spokesman for Christianity, whether we like it or not. So they came to Assisi, a very remarkable representation, which was not given as much coverage in this country as in others. The sheer fact of this historic world gathering deserves our praise to our friends in the Vatican, and our continued support.

We need ways to focus the fact that we live in one world, and express this within the Christian Churches. Of course we should take pride in our national story and the urgency of our mission to our own people. But I have been distressed to hear some criticisms of the ARCIC report which suggest a kind of autonomous, isolated, British Christianity. Augustine of

---

[1] Speech in the General Synod on 13 November 1986 during the debate on the Response to the Report of the Anglican–Roman Catholic International Commission.

Canterbury knew better. So did Theodore of Tarsus who gave shape to the Church of England – and so did Cranmer and the Reformers, who drew so much of their theology from Wittenberg and Geneva.

Today, our own experience of the Anglican Communion teaches us something of that catholicity of the Church. Its universality in time and space is one of the marks of the Church. Our contacts with the Roman Catholic Church bring this home forcibly, for Rome is pre-eminently an international Church. In Assisi I think of the modest contingent of two cardinals from each continent who joined the Pope as host to the other Churches and religions. I also think of the Pope inviting the Argentine Cardinal and Cardinal Basil Hume to celebrate Mass with him in St Peter's on the eve of his visit to this country and at the height of the Falklands crisis. This has nothing to do with political sovereignty; it has everything to do with the universality of the Kingdom of God.

My assistant, Terry Waite, who recently described himself as 'a mote or a beam always in the public eye', wins international attention and respect because he is perceived as someone not with the credentials of office or denomination but with the universal appeal of God's justice and Christ's compassion for the captive. It is perhaps worth mentioning that, as an Anglican layman, before he worked at Lambeth he had worked for seven years, based in Rome, for an international agency of the Roman Catholic Church.

Secondly, I want to speak about styles of authority. People still darkly purvey the myth that Rome never changes. I sometimes wonder whether people who say this have ever met some of my Roman Catholic friends in places where I was brought up, like Liverpool, and have any idea of the extraordinary upheaval caused to lay people, religious, priests and bishops by what we perhaps rather glibly call Vatican II. But myths about people are pretty impervious to correction if we take care never to meet them in a way in which we are open to their insights and correction, and they to ours. The Anglican Reformers would to a man have denied Rome's immutability. Their argument was precisely that Rome *had* changed. But so often our fixed views about the Catholic–Protestant debate have been formed by 19th century Anglo-Catholic/Evangelical polemics, rather than the real debates of the 16th and 17th centuries. At Assisi at least I did see the possibility of a new style of papal leadership, an ARCIC primacy rather than a papal monarchy. Pope John Paul was our host, and he welcomed us as such. But then he became, in his own words, 'a brother among brothers'. (Actually, there were some sisters there too, including the only other representative from this country, Val Ferguson of the Society of Friends.) Great care was taken to emphasize our fraternity rather than our hierarchy. We stood in a semi-circle and there was a careful allocation of readings and prayers to all. The Pope's chair was the same as everybody else's. We all bundled into the same bus, and the Pope had to look for a seat.

When it came to prayer in the presence of those of other faiths, the Pope went to great lengths to respect the integrity of the other world religions, and yet he was an authentic spokesman for Christianity in his unequivocal adherence to the Christian revelation. His address, the Christian contribution in the presence of other world faiths, began, 'I profess here anew my conviction, shared by all Christians, that in Jesus Christ, as Saviour of all, true peace is to be found . . . peace for me bears the name of Jesus Christ'.

Cynics can say that a change in style costs nothing. I am not sure. Among the Christian leaders present I had an interesting conversation with Emilio Castro, an evangelical, General Secretary of the World Council of Churches, who incidentally will be visiting the British Council later this month. Emilio, a Latin American if ever there was one, was telling me of Latin American satisfaction with the latest Vatican declaration on liberation theology – satisfaction among both Catholic and Protestant theologians. The first statement had been based on hearsay and hardly understood the Christian struggle in Latin America, where Brazil alone is the largest national Catholic Church in the world. The second Vatican statement was from the inside and has won respect. It is an open secret that the Brazilian bishops sent a delegation of their number to Rome earlier this year to explain their position and to make sure that Rome got it right. From this dialogue a new document emerged. A new, ARCIC-style primacy is thinkable. We must press for it by similar dialogue.

In the meantime, we need to be more aware of the danger of expecting perfection in others and failing to notice the warts in our own structures. The story of the beam and the mote has ecumenical significance as well as personal relevance. Of course there are serious problems. There are problems about the plight, for example, of some of the more outspoken liberal theologians: but do we not have the same troubles in this Synod? Having said that, I know well that there will be considerable anxiety about the ARCIC report. I respect the serious and good contribution which has been made during the course of this debate on Scripture, primacy and the place of the laity. Since one of the discoveries of modern Anglicanism has been the value of the voice of the laity in Church government, I shall be supporting a motion in this interest which is to follow, and I hope it will be accepted. I believe that the present ARCIC dialogue will welcome it as making much more explicit what earlier talks called the balance between conciliarity and primacy. It offers a real way forward.

I will conclude by urging those who have reservations to remember that love casts out fear. The ARCIC process is designed to create a new relationship between the Churches of the Anglican Communion and the Roman Catholic Church. Let us look forward to continuing the debate, but within a new relationship. Was the papal visit to Canterbury not signalling such a new relationship? And would any present on that day not long to pick it up and take it further for the unity of Christ's glorious Church? An Archbishop of Canterbury cannot but have respect for the Pope who sent Augustine to England, a Pope who exercised the sort of primacy that ARCIC commends to us today. Gregory the Great asked for 'no honour which shall detract from the honour of belonging to my brethren' and believed that it was 'through humility rather than supremacy that the unity of the Church is preserved'.

I urge the Synod to vote to continue our discussion with the Roman Catholic Church about such a primacy, a primacy which Gregory always described as that of *servus servorum Dei*, servant of the servants of God.

Conception of the Blessed Virgin Mary

ECUMENICAL PRUDENCE MIGHT have dissuaded the Archbishop of Canterbury from preaching[1] on the Feast of the Immaculate Conception. After all, it is claimed that the Marian Dogmas are one of the issues which divide us. But English bishops have not recently been well known for their silence and ecumenical dialogue must always mean speaking the truth in love. In fact there are compelling historical reasons why an Archbishop of Canterbury can hardly avoid the subject if he has travelled from Lyon to the monastery of his predecessor, St Anselm, at about this time of year.

Tomorrow's Feast – known in the Anglican Book of Common Prayer simply as the Conception of the Blessed Virgin Mary – was known in the Christian East from the seventh century. It was probably brought by pilgrims to Saxon England before the Norman Conquest. Its first liturgical occurrence in the West is found in an Anglo-Saxon Benedictional from Canterbury Cathedral. In France the feast first spread to Lyon due to English influence, where it was defended against no less a person than St Bernard by an English bishop who originally came from St Albans – my former diocese. But the feast only became universally accepted against the views of theologians such as Albert the Great and Thomas Aquinas through the immense reputation of Anselm. Or rather through his name. For it was his biographer, Eadmer, the monk of Canterbury, who patriotically wrote in defence of the Anglo-Saxon custom of keeping the Feast of the Conception which had been suppressed by the Normans. This defence by Eadmer was later assumed to be by Anselm himself. Disciple was confused with master.

Our feast, therefore, is of distinctly English origin. Not that it was always accepted by later English theologians. There is the fourteenth century story of an Oxford lecturer who refused to consider the eighth of December a holiday and wanted to teach as

[1] Address at the Abbey of le Bec Helluoin in Normandy, on 7 December 1984.

usual. Every year, however, he was struck down by illness on the feast day until, so the tale goes – a Cambridge tale by the way – he eventually took the point and accepted the doctrine.

So much for its historical origins. But what does it actually *mean*? What Christian *truth* lies behind the devotion? And does this *divide* Anglicans and Roman Catholics?

I do not want to enter the very long and learned debates about the doctrine from the late Middle Ages onwards. In any case, the parameters of that discussion were set by Anselm and Eadmer themselves. Anselm is clear that even the most privileged of the human race had been born with the taint common to all mankind: 'The Virgin herself was conceived "in iniquity, and in sin did her mother conceive her", and she was born with original sin, for she also sinned in Adam "in whom all have sinned".' Anselm saw with clear sight that the whole economy of redemption depended on the inescapable transmission of original sin through the act of conception. If the link between conception could be broken in one case then the necessity of Christ as redeemer of the whole human race would be jeopardized. Eadmer, on the contrary, defending the Canterbury devotion to the Conception, argued that God *could* grant that the Virgin should be conceived without sin; that if he *could* he *would* and that what he could and would he *did*. And so the argument has continued till modern times.

The arguments for and against presuppose a strongly Augustinian notion of original sin contracted by human procreation. Both the point and objections to the doctrine lose coherence if this is questioned, and of course it is questioned by contemporary Christians who do not doubt the reality of original sin, but who do reject the biological formulation of the doctrine the West has inherited from St Augustine. No one living in the last quarter of the twentieth century can doubt the flawed nature of humanity and its propensity for evil choices rather than good. But the Augustinian theory of its transmission is another matter. As a consequence the *meaning* of the doctrine of Mary's immaculate conception is also in doubt.

I also spoke of the *truth* behind the doctrine and devotion. Here we are dealing with something ultimately more important than its verbal formulation. The Anglican–Roman Catholic International Commission has spoken of agreement in the recognition of 'the grace and unique vocation of Mary, Mother of God Incarnate (Theotokos)' and 'that she was prepared by divine grace to be the mother of our Redeemer, by whom she was herself redeemed and received into glory'. The heart of the matter is our common belief that Mary was chosen by God to be the instrument – through her free will – of the incarnation. And she whom God chose he also prepared by grace. So Mary is a sign of God's preparatory grace before the birth of Christ. The long line of preparation for the Christ event is of grace. The chosen land, the chosen people, Moses and the Prophets, the forerunner John the Baptist: all disclose the traces of grace and glory. In Mary the preparation reaches its graceful climax.

This is the truth we celebrate today – a truth which unites us. A common truth grounded in the mystery of the incarnation, which right belief in Mary protects and defends. In the security of this common truth we can echo Anselm's poetry when he says:

> Mother of the life of my soul,
> nurse of the redeemer of my flesh,
> who gave suck to the Saviour of my whole being . . .
> O woman, uniquely to be wondered at,
> and to be wondered at for your uniqueness,
> by you the elements are renewed, hell is redeemed,
> demons are trampled down and men are saved.[2]

And we can pray Anselm's prayer:

> Dear Lord, spare the servant of your mother; dear Lady, spare the servant of your son.[3]

---

[2] *The Prayers and Meditations of Saint Anselm* trans. Sister Benedicta Ward, SLG (Penguin Books, 1973) pp. 116, 119–20.
[3] Ibid p. 112.

In South Africa

🙪🙪🙪🙪

PEACE BE WITH you – from God our Father and the Lord Jesus Christ. It is good for us to be here.[1] It is good to share with you in this Eucharist of Celebration. I am here as your guest, with many others, to represent the Anglican Communion on this historic day. That is a reminder to us that we are part of one world-wide Church. When one part rejoices, we all rejoice. When one part suffers, we all suffer. Along with us are many from other religious traditions. The things which unite us are greater than anything which divides us. We want you to know that we are with you today, and will stand by you in future. That is why we are here.

All the world is watching and listening. Our friends everywhere are praying for us now as Desmond Tutu becomes Archbishop of Cape Town – the first to come from the black people who form the majority of this Province.

We know him to be a man of God. He has stayed in my home, so I know he gets up earlier than I do to say his prayers. He is a man of the people. You have freely elected him. He has not been imposed on you. You have a Xhosa proverb: 'UMFUNDISI NGUMFUNDISI NGABANTU' ('A priest is only a priest through his people.') His laughter and spontaneity can sometimes upset the pompous and shock the solemn. As they said of Jesus, 'He doesn't speak like a religious official'.

Desmond is a man of love, vision and peace, whose valiant stand for Christ has brought such life and hope to South Africa, and far beyond. I believe you have a leader chosen by God, to transcend the honest differences of the people of this province from the Cape to the northern borders of Namibia and Mozambique. Hold him and his wife Leah in your prayers.

I come not simply to pay a tribute to a friend, not only to encourage him with the massive support he has from the

---

[1] Sermon preached at a concelebrated Eucharist held in the Goodwood Stadium, Cape Town, South Africa, on Sunday 7 September 1986.

international community – certainly not to give him advice. I come to preach the gospel (the good news of Jesus Christ) because it brings a shaft of light into our troubled times. You have just heard the Easter story. It tells of a God who, when human possibilities are exhausted, acts beyond our hoping and gives beyond our asking. Consider that moving little sentence in the story: 'Mary Magdalene stood at the tomb weeping.'[2]

All of us here today who rejoice at this magnificent service know too the tears which Mary wept. Hers was a sorrow that weighs down our hearts too – the sorrow of bereavement, bewilderment, even despair. Mary had known the suffering that many among her people, perhaps as always the women most of all, had to bear. She had shared in their oppression – oppression which then, as now, carries its victims into exile or captivity. Husbands separated from wives, children taken from parents. Mary knew the pressure of poverty. She endured the agony of injustice which cuts people off from each other, and makes slaves of them. And Mary's hopes had been raised so high, just as ours can be. Jesus came moving among his people with words of wisdom and acts of love, setting their hearts alight with power to heal and restore. He brought promise of a new freedom, which the Old Testament prophets had long foretold. He offered a different kind of life. Before his authority, police, soldiers and rulers seemed confused.

We have seen in our day, and all over the world, those imprisoned for their loyalty to truth who stand out as he did with courage and dignity. They win the reluctant respect of their captors. They are free of fear or guilt, free of hatred or bitterness. They become the real judges of the world.

What terrible sorrow and void there is when such a light as this seems to be extinguished, crushed, destroyed. Death and darkness smother the last glimmer of hope. Only despair remains. With such despair, Mary wept. And we weep with her. But even in such moments of darkness (when we seem blinded by tears) the wondrous light which broke in upon Mary with the first dawn of that new day breaks upon us now.

At first there was just the stirring of people somewhere far off. Figures in white were speaking to her. Beside the tomb a gardener was asking what was wrong, trying to bring comfort.

[2] John 20.11.

Then came the voice – strange yet somehow familiar. A voice you never seemed to have heard before and yet have always known, a voice that calls you by your name: 'Mary!' All at once she recognized that presence. This is no stranger's voice: 'Rabboni! Master!'. 'I have seen the Lord', she told the disciples.

The theme of death and resurrection lies deep in human experience. Not only in our own lives; but in the lives of nations. Here in South Africa an old order is dying. As we watch, we experience all the agony, doubt and uncertainty which surround death. But if we have faith, we know that beyond death lies the assurance of resurrection.

We can see now that Jesus has brought to us all the power in faith to lay down our life, so that it can be taken up again. Trusting in him alone we can surrender our lives, to find ourselves afresh. A new freedom is released in the midst of this world, the power of God that can never be suppressed. This is the heart of our gospel.

We must be ready now, at this moment in human history, confronted anew by the same true and living Christ, to surrender ourselves. That means those who *hold* power in this world must be ready to renounce it for the sake of Christ. And, in the same way, those who seek power must be ready, even after all they have suffered, to make room for the claims of people they have seen as oppressors. Those who fear for their safety or for their rights must be ready to risk all for his sake. Those of us in the West who have done much to create this present tragic situation here must be ready to repent and change and make sacrifices. I want you to know I believe this is happening and all our churches long to know how we can help. I come to tell you in their name and in the name of Christ that we support you in your struggle to create a united South Africa out of the divisive forces which hold you in their grip. But I do not want to speak smooth words of peace where there is no peace.

A person precariously balanced on top of a pile of logs is aware of the hurt that will be done if it collapses. Not surprisingly he calls for stability, for change that is gentle. A person who is squeezed under the pile of logs is conscious of his present pain. He calls out to be freed, even if it brings down the whole pile. As no system based on brutal repression can endure, so no change achieved by violence can escape its damaging infection. These are the lessons of history. They are the message of the cross.

We must grieve over all victims of violence and cruelty. But the Church must not be owned, possessed, or manipulated either to bolster up a system which is unchristian, or to serve a political ideology which leaves out God.

The risen Christ wills us to go and tell our brothers and sisters the truth of his Lordship through self-giving, to show his life through death. He opens up before us the new relationship with God and with each other into which he would draw us all. He would bring each and all of us into his new Kingdom-community in the Spirit, where there is no room for greed or possessiveness, where perfect love casts out fear.

The only way is a way of painful repentance and costly love. There are no short cuts. Once take that way of the cross and beyond it lies a vision of a new heaven and a new earth – a Kingdom into which can come all the nations of this world, yes, all this beautiful South Africa with its rich human and material resources.

Our witness must be to that Christ who is the fulfilment of the hope of every faith, and the good dreams of every culture. Christ is the inspiration of those of all races who have fought, in the words of Nelson Mandela, 'against white domination and against black domination and who have cherished the ideal of a domestic and free society, a happy place for all peoples'.

There have always been those in the Churches of South Africa who have borne true witness to this ideal and given themselves wholly for it in the freedom of faith. There were missionaries, African prophets, ordinary Christians who envisaged this shared life in the Spirit. Church leaders have been raised up again and again to continue that teaching. You can name them better than I. Some should be here today and they are not. I cannot fail to mention Sigisbert, Bishop Suffragan of Johannesburg, that gentle bishop of our Church.

Today, Desmond Tutu, who stands in that great succession, has been enthroned as Archbishop at this critical moment in the life of this nation. He has been raised up in this generation as a witness to the real power and purpose of God in Christ. I well remember *his* message to the Church of England earlier this year. It rings true to the theme and goal of his life: 'We want to be freed – but with the whites.' If all of us, black and white, are ready for a real turning to God, then the infinite power of faith and freedom can be released in the Church and in the world.

The way of the cross is a sign of hope and an answer to sorrow. But it also asks questions of each of *us*: it demands to know by what right we call ourselves Christians.

Here in South Africa, in a religious country, the questions posed by the cross have a resonance perhaps greater than anywhere in the world. As I stand here on the tip of Africa, I cannot escape the sense of history unfolding – the sense that here on what was once called the Dark Continent there is the threat of greater darkness still.

There is a moment in the lives of all of us, and of all nations, when we have to choose, finally, between the way of life and the way of death. Which is the way for South Africa? Is the way of violence the way of life or death – be the violence perpetrated by the state or practised by the individual? Is imprisonment and torture the way to freedom and peace? Or does it lead instead to anger, frustration and despair? Which way are South Africans choosing?

I hear the voices of those who yearn for peace; but I hear as loudly those who seem to long for blood and war. Those voices are heard from all communities. The way to bridge this gulf is the Christian way of self-giving repentance, the way of generosity, the way of love and life itself.

The way of the cross means readiness to talk and listen, even when words appear empty. To talk of the future when it is tempting to dwell in the past. To reason when others choose rhetoric. To stay calm when others counsel war. The Christian way shows us too that words alone are not enough. They must spring from a Christ-like spirit of love, compassion and understanding.

The world is looking today to South Africa for signs of this spirit. They are looking for a miracle. Such a miracle always involves risk. Here in this part of Africa we see most sharply the problems which face us in every part of our world. They can be summarized in one simple question from the Gospel: 'How is it possible to love my neighbour as myself?'

So, on this enthronement day we, neighbours to each other, give thanks for Desmond, and pray for God's blessing on this Church and on this beloved country. We know that however much we may be separated from one another – by the oceans of the world, by the laws of the land, or by prison bars – nothing can ever separate us from the love of God in Christ Jesus our Lord:

not persecution or affliction, nothing in the world as it is, or as it shall be, nothing in death or life. We know that in the end our resurrection faith will triumph, and transform the kingdoms of this world into the Kingdom of our Lord and Saviour, Jesus Christ.

One hundred years ago a preacher in my own land, Hugh Price Hughes,[3] sounded this true note of Christian hope: 'If you ever hear anybody saying that slavery is inevitable, war is inevitable, poverty is inevitable, you can shout out: "Thank God that's a lie! Jesus Christ lives and shall bring it about that right shall utterly prevail."' In that confident faith we shall share the bread and cup of this sacrament, and pray that Christ may be enthroned in all our hearts, for he is our God, for time and for eternity.

---

[3] 1847–1902, president of the Wesleyan Conference.

Meeting of Faiths

THANK YOU FOR welcoming me to your group.[1] I am happy to meet representatives from so many different religions. We come together in a spirit of friendship and dialogue to share experiences and insights from our different faiths. I am in India as a guest, happy to be here again after an earlier visit many years ago. However, I have not only come as a guest but as a pilgrim, in a spirit of openness and enquiry, willing to learn from what I see and experience here, ready to ask what we can share in each other.

We all know that dialogue between members of different faiths is, historically speaking, a very recent development. In the past - and unfortunately not only in the past - members of different religions, or even from different branches within the same religion, have often met each other more in a spirit of opposition and exclusion rather than in a spirit of reconciliation and friendship. By now the various experiments in dialogue have come a long way - although not necessarily far enough - in the recognition that other faiths than our own are genuine homes of the spirit with many mansions to be discovered rather than solitary fortresses to be attacked.

As a Christian I welcome the spirit of openness and encounter, the generous hospitality of Indians, the spirit of human warmth and friendship, and above all the great religious heritage found here.

Our attitude in turn implies an openness to listen, a willingness to learn and reconsider, and to respond to what we encounter. We come with a sincerity of heart and the genuine desire to be open to the spiritual insights and experiences present in the many different communities of faith living here, but also with the practical concerns of our common humanity uppermost in our mind.

What can Western Christians learn from the experiences and insights of the different religions practised in India today? Many

---

[1] Address to leaders of many faiths at Bishop's House, Calcutta, 13 February 1986.

people have reflected and written at length on this question to which a great many answers can be given. I would like to single out three points for brief comment: we can learn from India something about the understanding and practice of religious pluralism; we can be particularly enriched and inspired by the Indian experience of the divine; and we can also learn something about the life of the spirit within us and relate this to a much needed practical spirituality in the contemporary world.

First some words about pluralism and the need for dialogue. We live today in a world of unprecedented ethnic, social, cultural and religious pluralism; a situation which creates new opportunities and new problems for all of us. For centuries India has witnessed the coexistence of many different ethnic and religious groups. Hindus, Buddhists, Jains and Sikhs have India as their land of origin, but from an early age members of other religious communities came from the outside and settled here too. Christians, Parsis, Muslims and Jews – so that we find an extraordinary mosaic of faiths throughout the Indian subcontinent.

Today's global situation of religious pluralism should be seen as an important opportunity for mutual enrichment rather than for communal tension. We must explore together the specific insights, the moments of revelation and disclosure, the spiritual treasures which our respective faiths have accumulated and handed down from generation to generation, whereby the lives of countless people have been nourished, sustained and transformed; today as in the past. If we are honest with each other, as we must be, we will recognize our profound diversities in belief and practice, and this can be a deeply painful experience. There are not only differences between our various religions, but there also exists pluralism within each of our own communities of faith. There are different kinds of Hinduism, of Buddhism, of Jainism, Islam, Sikhism, and so on, just as there are many different historical and theological strands within Christianity. Yet we recognize today that each faith possesses an irreplaceable spiritual heritage, a specific message and distinctive identity of its own which is of tremendous importance for all of us. We must be humble and sincere enough to concede that there is some incompleteness and shortcoming in each of our traditions; that there is room and need for further growth in all of them.

The encounter of world religions – of people from different faiths – is a global event of historical importance. We, as people of faith, owe it to the world to respond to the challenge of contemporary religious pluralism, not by weakening the intensity of our religious commitment, but through entering into dialogue at the deepest level by strengthening the depth of our faith, by renewing the sincerity of our worship and by increasing the fervour of our spirituality.

The World Council of Churches has actively promoted interreligious dialogue since 1967. Because of its history, and because its people belong to so many different faiths, India is particularly well placed to make dialogue possible and actively encourage its further development. Christians from many different Churches have been involved in some of the pioneering efforts of developing dialogue in India. Through their active involvement they have been greatly enriched and in turn have raised new questions about the Christian understanding of God and the world.

This brings me to my second point, the Indian experience of the divine, from which Christians can learn a great deal. The rich religious life of India is like a prism of many colours, or like a bridge which links the human and divine poles of our existence, often in ways different from Christianity, and yet in many respects it can deeply enrich and strengthen our Christian conception of God.

The religions of India have found many names for God, many faces and forms of expression for the ultimate mystery, the One and the All, the spirit which animates, pervades and sustains everything in existence. The longing of the human heart, of all our hearts, seeks to find this ultimate mystery in the midst of life and far beyond it. To find the invisible behind the visible, the everlasting behind the everchanging turmoils of this world and our own being is the great hope of the human heart. We all yearn for peace, salvation and fulfilment, for the plenitude of the spirit promised to us, summed up in India in the one word *Brahman* which stands for pure being, consciousness and joy. Although we all come from different religious backgrounds, we can all recognize a prayer of profound longing and hope in the well-known invocation of the Upanishads:

> Lead me from the Unreal to the Real,
> From Darkness to Light,
> From Death to Immortality.

Indian religious life presents us with an amazing variety of perspectives on the divine spirit as source of all life, whether this spirit is celebrated as utterly impersonal transcendence, worshipped as lord of all beings, meditated upon as innermost centre of human person, or praised as a loving God of grace.

When Thomas Merton came to India, he reflected on the spiritual significance of his pilgrimage to this country, as you can read in his *Asian Journal*,[2] where he especially describes his encounter and dialogue with Hindus and Buddhists. Merton felt that Hinduism was vibrating with a God-consciousness as presence – God not primarily understood as concept or image, but encountered in the fulness of experience as ultimate ground of reality and meaning from which all life and love flows.

Some years ago the Anglican theologian, Bishop John Robinson, wrote a book about the encounter of Hinduism and Christianity which he entitled *Truth is Two-Eyed*.[3] Given the richness and diversity of Indian religious perspectives, it might be rather more appropriate to say, drawing on a well-known Indian image, that the 'truth is thousand-eyed' in order to express the realization that the fulness of truth is reflected for us in myriads of facets and faces, all of which the unfathomable mystery of the divine must encompass in ways that surpass our understanding. This irreducible mystery can only be reverently approached in prayer, meditation, worship and praise; it often finds a powerful symbolic expression in many of our places of worship and shrines, whether they be Hindu, Muslim, Sikh, Buddhist or Christian.

For Christians, the person of Jesus Christ, his life and suffering remain the primary source of knowledge and truth about God. The central message of the Christian gospel is a message of love; love poured out in the radical self giving of God in his Son for the sake of all creation, for the whole world and every being within it; a message of death and resurrection for the salvation of all. Yet Christians recognize that other faiths reveal other aspects of God which may well enrich and enlarge our own understanding.

The Christian monk Swami Abhishiktananda has said that India's heritage is Christ's also and her treasures have to be

---

[2] Sheldon Press, 1973.
[3] SCM Press, 1979.

shared by his Church. Others have spoken of the need to immerse the Church in the realities of Asia so that the Christian message of love and liberation becomes freed from its 'Western bondage'. There is no easy way forward in these matters, but the 'Church has to be truly incarnate in the life and thought forms of India. The utter simplicity of much of Indian life, especially in the villages and among the poor, can remind Christians more than any other experience, of their original calling to a spirit of service, love and communion. Is Jesus not a man of suffering, the sign of hope for the poor and downtrodden, the strength of the weak, the helper of the needy, the 'prince of peace' as the Church calls him in her liturgy? Many years ago Eli Stanley Jones wrote a book called *The Christ on the Indian Road*,[4] an image which conveys a profound truth for Christians, as Christ is found on all roads; but this title reminds us also of our pilgrimage together with all fellowmen in need.

We are all called to love and service, but this requires the overcoming of many obstacles which still exist between us as well as in our own hearts. We must overcome anger, hatred and greed, as the Buddhists say, in order to practise compassion for all sentient beings and revere all life. To be sincere with each other and open to each other's needs, we must be attentive to the call of the spirit within us, the source of all energy and renewal.

This brings me to my last point: what can we learn from India about the life of the spirit, and how we can relate this to a practical spirituality in response to the needs of the contemporary world.

The Indian religious heritage contains a great variety of spiritual disciplines and knows many saints and sages; great spiritual teachers who lived and taught the path of meditation and inwardness. Indian spirituality invites Christians perhaps above all to greater inwardness, to the practice of contemplation and meditation, to a life of inner and outer simplicity. Many Western Christians have come to India to learn precisely this, to be schooled in the inner life. It is quite remarkable how many Christian ashrams have been founded all over India in a few decades. Members from all the different Christian groups are taking part in this, whether Orthodox Syrian or Mar Thoma Christians, Protestants or Roman Catholics, and there are some ecumenical ashrams too.

---

[4] Hodder and Stoughton, 1926.

It gives me particular pleasure to recall that one of the first Christian ashrams was the *Christa Seva Sangh Ashram* founded in Pune in 1927 by the Anglican Franciscan, Father Jack Winslow. It was his ideal to adapt the Indian cultural heritage to a Christian life style and witness and to introduce certain Indian features into Christian worship. Father Winslow was experimenting at the practical level at a time when Roman Catholics such as Father Johanns and others explored Christian adaptations of the Indian heritage at the level of theological thought. The Indian expressions of Christian worship and theology have come a long way since then and are far too numerous to be even mentioned here, but perhaps I should just say that Father Winslow's foundation continues to exist today as an ecumenical ashram where Roman Catholics, Anglicans, members of the Church of North India and Hindus live and pray together.

Many experiments are taking place in the area of spirituality today and there is certainly much for us to learn from Indian spirituality. Yet one must also be cautious not to overstate a few selective features and exaggerate the claims of Indian spirituality in a one-sided, exclusive manner, as has sometimes happened. Spirituality must never be taken out of its fuller human context. True spirituality belongs to the whole person, inward and outward, and must be transformative of all aspects of life. It must be practically oriented, towards justice and peace, the building of community, and towards helping the suffering and the poor.

Modern Indian cities are not much different from cities in the West in that they too can become places of desolation and despair where it is difficult for the young, the destitute, the hungry, to discover *any* life of the spirit. All spirituality must be truly incarnational and practical, and must be judged by its fruits. In other words, spirituality must always be related to a responsible social ethic.

While Christians may strive for greater inwardness, contemporary Indians are actively engaged in moving outwards, into the areas of social and political action, in the affirmation of their distinct cultural and national identity, the building of nationhood, and in working for greater social and economic justice. This requires a certain kind of dialogue, too, so that harmony and balance are maintained between the different ethnic and religious groups.

Modern India has given the world a great example of the right spirit of dialogue in the person of Mahatma Gandhi. He was willing to learn from all the religions of his land and draw on their heritage in his worship and work. He truly practised the spirit of radical love and service and followed the call of truth in his actions for the suffering and poor, for the sake of all Indians, whether Hindus, Muslims, Sikhs, Christians, Jains, Jews or Parsis. In many ways very traditional and orthodox, he retained his deep identity as a Hindu and yet was one of the most radical reformers and innovators too. Many English Christians were inspired early on by Gandhi's ideas as these became widely known in England through Gandhi's close friendship with C F Andrews.[5]

Gandhi's shining example can be an inspiration for dialogue in action, not merely in words, by entering dialogue as an experience which involves risk and adventure, and the humility to recognize one's utter vulnerability. One of the main obstacles to genuine dialogue is the feeling of superiority – of the superiority of one's own faith, of one's particular spirituality or religious practice, and also the fear to lose one's own identity. We must be aware of our own distinctive centre, but be able to grow outward and upward in the spirit of equal partnership. Dialogue in depth is rooted in and nourished by the interiority of its participants. In the course of any genuine dialogue we all both give and receive until we reach a depth of communion never shared before.

Thus we need to reflect on the most appropriate environment for dialogue; we need to foster dialogue at the deepest level of experience where we encounter authentic, self-manifesting spirituality which can feed and sustain the *élan* of both our inner and outer life. This requires an effort of mind and will and, most of all, a preparation of the heart. Only then can we become truly receptive to the life of the spirit in our midst.

Christians see in the encounter between people of different faiths a sign of God's will in changing social and political circumstances. All religious people ultimately trust in a higher and stronger power than that of human beings to direct our search and growth and strengthen our efforts. Today, more than ever before, we are called to make an act of faith in the

---

[5] 1870–1940. Initially a member of the Cambridge Mission to Delhi, he devoted his life to the service of India and the cause of Indian nationalism.

transcendent and to be inspired by the promise which interreligious dialogue as a new fruit of the spirit presents to us in the midst of human encounter. Such promise holds much hope for our torn world, especially the hope for peace and greater unity.

May our efforts in dialogue strengthen the bonds of fellowship between us and make us grow in the spirit of truth and love.

Thanksgiving in Shanghai

As LEADER OF the British Council of Churches delegation, it is my privilege to reply to the speech of welcome given by my friend and brother, Bishop Ting.[1]

First, in the name of the whole delegation, I wish to give thanks for our safe arrival after what seems like a very long journey. Our thanksgiving is deepened, however, by the reflection that our journey was infinitely shorter than those of the travellers who have preceded us. I think of Olopan, Marco Polo and Matteo Ricci, and even Hewlett Johnson, the Dean of Canterbury and my friend Joseph Needham. We are not-so-wise men and women from the West, come with all the benefits of air travel, and we give thanks for the ease and speed of our journey.

The journey itself gave us an opportunity to grow into Christian friendship with one another and to prepare ourselves spiritually for our visit to China. The experience caused us to reflect on the great history of memorable journeys in the Scriptures. The very first words of the very first Creed in the Old Testament are devoted to this theme – a wandering Aramean was my father. We remember Abraham, the exodus of the children of Israel, their exile; our Lord's journey to Jerusalem – all these journeys produced new understanding of God, the traveller left the familiar and became vulnerable to the new light which God wished to show him. The travellers became pilgrims and I have no hesitation in describing this journey as a pilgrimage of deep spiritual significance. We have travelled full of hope and full of expectation in this season of Advent, looking to receive much from our visit here. Already we have been overwhelmed and moved by the warmth of our welcome. Chinese Christians, I know from the past, are, as St Paul recommends in our lesson,[2] 'given to hospitality'.

---

[1] Sermon at Mo-en church on 3 December 1983 at the Service of Thanksgiving for safe arrival in Shanghai.
[2] Romans 12.1–18.

Thanksgiving in Shanghai

Christianity has a very long history in China. Only forty years after the arrival of the first Archbishop of Canterbury in England, a Christian priest made the first recorded missionary journey to China. We give thanks for the history of Christian faith in this land, but we also accept judgement of their history. Too often Christianity has been confined to foreign and minority cultures or worse, Christian missionaries have tried to make Chinese men and women into imitation Europeans. We give honour to those who did not follow this way, to men like Matteo Ricci who left their own homes in the West and became Chinese themselves in order to reveal the face of the God of love in this land. But now we have much more reason for thanksgiving in the achievements of the Three-Self Movement in creating an authentic Chinese Church, full of lively Christians who are also loyal citizens of the People's Republic, stirred by their convictions about the God and Father of our Lord Jesus Christ to be particularly energetic and positive members of the community. Thank God no one can now repeat the slur, 'One Christian more, one Chinese less'.

We come here knowing a number of you already and looking forward with eager expectation to making many more friends. We already apply to you so many of the descriptive phrases in Paul's letter to the Romans. When I hear the words, 'not slothful in business, fervent in spirit, serving the Lord', I remember Bishop Ting, Han Wen Zao and the other members of the China Christian Council in their journeys and their meetings around the world, establishing friendships on the basis of mutual respect. Knowing as I do something of the many calls on their skill and their love, it is a wonder that they have achieved so much in such a short time and yet show so little sign of strain.

I think also of the words, 'rejoicing in hope, patient in tribulation, continuing steadfast in prayer'. In common with much of Chinese society, Chinese Christians have suffered a very great deal for their faithfulness to their ideals. The liveliness of Christian life and the numbers of Churches at the present time in China is nothing short of a contemporary Christian miracle. Faith tested by what St Paul calls 'tribulation' has great power. In China we have seen this power in our own days, and it gives us hope. I thank God for a Church which is able to use the words, 'Bless them which persecute you, bless and curse not', knowing their full cost and knowing their full power to transform life with love and to redeem the most desperate situations.

We come, therefore, above all to share the riches of our faith as brothers and sisters, giving thanks for all that we have received from the Lord Jesus Christ who belongs to no one culture as its exclusive property but who is in all and above all, who is to be worshipped in every tongue and in every place on earth and in heaven. I thank our Chinese hosts for the appropriate way in which they have permitted us to begin this visit, because the Christian prayer of thanksgiving is one of the great transforming influences in the world.

So many of our contemporaries attempt to live as if they were the centre of life. Inevitably they come into conflict with others who also regard themselves as the centre. There is conflict and violence in the struggle for supremacy. It is true on an individual level, it is true on the level of groups and nations. If Christians train themselves in thanksgiving, they come to see more and more deeply that there is only one true centre to life: God the author and giver of all things. They come to see life as a gift and an expression of the love that God has for mankind. It was this kind of thanksgiving that moved our Lord even in the night that he was betrayed. He took up the elements of life, bread and wine. He gave thanks over them. He referred them to God the giver. He revealed them as expressions of the divine love for us, and so he received them back charged with a new power. The bread and wine, after the prayer of thanksgiving, is no longer the food which merely sustains our existence. It is heavenly bread and the cup of salvation which unites us with the love and life of God himself, through his Son Jesus Christ.

Thanks be to God for all his mercies, for setting us upon this road, and for bringing us here to China among Christian brothers and sisters. Amen.